THE
STREET
SMART
SALES PRO

THE
STREET
SMART
SALES PRO

HOW TO CREATE, INFLUENCE, AND CLOSE ANY SALE

ARTHUR ROGEN

SQUAREONE
PUBLISHERS

COVER DESIGNER: Jeannie Tudor
TYPESETTER: Gary A. Rosenberg

Square One Publishers
115 Herricks Road
Garden City Park, NY 11040
(516) 535-2010 • (877) 900-BOOK
www.squareonepublishers.com

Library of Congress Cataloging-in-Publication Data

Rogen, Arthur.
  [Street smart salesman]
  Street smart sales pro : making opportunities happen / Arthur Rogen.
      pages cm
  Includes bibliographical references and index.
  ISBN 978-0-7570-0390-5
  1. Selling. I. Title.
  HF5438.25.R63 2013
  658.85—dc23
                              201302593

Printed in the United States of America

10   9   8   7   6   5   4   3   2   1

Contents

To the four jewels of my life.
To my wife, Sally,
who has always been the street smart driving force
behind all my successes.
To my daughters, Jennifer and Lisa,
who will always be Daddy's little girls
no matter how old they are.
To my son, Eric,
who has inspired me with his determination
and courage to succeed.

Acknowledgments

My thanks go first to Martin Rogen, my father. He gave me the confidence to believe in myself and not be afraid to achieve greatness. For that I will always be grateful.

My thanks also go to Eve Rogen, my mother. As I was growing up, she reinforced that my creativity and sense of humor were gifts, even when, at times, they got me into all sorts of mischief.

My thanks go to Abraham and Fanny Lefkowitz, my in-laws, who have made me feel more like a son than a son-in-law.

My thanks go to Rose Lippman, my aunt. How lucky I have been to have someone in my corner like her. Her love has never been taken for granted.

My thanks go to Robert Sunshine, my oldest friend. They say that if you have one friend in life that you can count on, it is a gift. Rob is that friend. Thank God he made the wise decision to marry Jane, whom both Sally and I equally love.

My thanks go to Ira and Jo Sirota, who have spent many an hour acting as sounding boards for my various ventures. I shall never forgive them for moving to Las Vegas.

My thanks go to Irv Torbin, who has been a trusted friend and confidant during the past twenty years.

My thanks go to Scott and Debbie Gutterson, Ruth and David Gantman, Laura and Gary Lefkowitz, Linda and Elliot Glasser, Roberta Kane, Toni and Fred Valenstein, Randy and Steve Galler, Gail and

Danny Katz, and Bob Greenspan, who have been there for me through thick and thin.

My thanks go to Hal Markowitz, Iris Levine, Roger Gilbert, Merrie Hollander, and Steve Finkelstein, who gave me street smart insight into the manuscript.

My thanks go to all the street smart sales pros whom I have met through the years who have made this book possible. Special thanks go to Larry Wilson and Gene Lloyd, who early on taught me that being in sales is being in the greatest profession of all.

Lastly, my thanks go to Rudy Shur at Square One Publishers, who is most responsible for *The Street Smart Sales Pro*. Without Rudy's patience, insight, and unfaltering confidence in my ability to write, I would never have been able to complete this book. His friendship is something that I will cherish forever.

Gender Bender

The fact is, a "pro" is as likely to be a female as a male. However, our language does not provide us with a genderless pronoun. To avoid using the awkward "he/she" or the impersonal "it" when referring to a salesperson, while still giving equal time to both sexes, the masculine "he," "him," and "his" have been used in odd-numbered chapters, while the feminine pronouns "she," "her," and "hers" appear in the rest. This decision was made in the interest of simplicity and clarity.

Foreword

As the publisher of this book, I would like to see every man, woman, and child in this country buy a copy of this title. Of course, I would like to see that happen with every one of my books, but the thing is I would never publicly say that—or have it printed in a foreword. Why? Because it might be considered embarrassing or brash. Some people think that it might not be appropriate for the person who published the book to proclaim that this is the very best book you will ever read on the art of selling. Well, maybe if I hadn't known Arthur Rogen, I would think the same way. But Art taught me never to be embarrassed about anything I was truly proud of. And I'm very proud of Art. Knowing him for over forty years has profoundly changed the way I market and sell books, and knowing Art has changed me as well.

A number of years back, my cousin Irv arranged for my wife and me to meet with another couple he thought we'd like to know, since we all lived in Flushing, New York. The husband was a teaching buddy of Irv; they both worked at the same school in the South Bronx. Irv thought since we were both young married couples, each with a baby girl, we might have a lot in common. It turned out he was right. I was working for a college textbook publisher as a commissioned sales rep, and he was looking to find another source of income to add to his teacher's salary. That summer, Art got a summer job selling real estate in Pennsylvania, and from that point on he never looked back.

Early on, I would listen to the many stories Art recounted about his experiences selling property. The way Art told them, these stories were not only hilarious, but ingenious. The things he did to get leads, the manner in which he would treat each prospect, and the ways he would get them to buy his lots of land—these were selling stories that truly boggled the mind. At times, Art could be outrageous, reserved, charming, or unpredictable—but he was always good hearted. As I watched his fortune quickly rise in the company he worked for, I could also see that he never acted impulsively. Rather, he always knew exactly what he was going to do. He had the ability to sense what the moment called for and acted accordingly. It seemed to me that he was a natural-born salesman—something I was not.

We spent a good deal of time discussing the process of selling—really, it was more like me asking questions and him answering them. Although he had stopped working in education, the teacher in him was always there. As I visited campus after campus in my job, trying to get professors to adopt my company's textbooks, there would come a moment during one of my presentations that I would think, "What would Artie do in this situation?" Then I'd remember something he told me, and proceed to do it—and just like that, I'd get a professor to commit to reviewing a book, if he didn't adopt it outright.

At a certain point in my career, I began to think about starting my own publishing company. I thought I was pretty good at what I did; I was young, and I really had no idea what I was about to get myself into, but I knew I had to try. After talking to my wife and getting her blessing, I quit the company for which I worked. The first thing I did then was to call Art and ask him if he would like to be my partner. I could think of no one who would be better at sales. Never having done anything like this before, I phoned Art and told him what I was going to do, at which point I blurted out, "And I would really like you to be my partner." There was silence. Considering that I had just asked another person to share the risks and successes that a new business venture might entail, dead silence on the other side of the receiver was not the kind of response I was hoping for.

Finally, he replied. "I can't believe two great minds think that much alike! I just bought a large parcel of land in upstate New York a few days ago, and I'm starting my own real estate company as well," he said. "If I hadn't done that, I would have absolutely said yes; you know that! Look, Rudy, if you have any questions that I can answer, or if you need any help, I'm here for you. And if you need a really nice piece of land located in the beautiful mountains of upstate New York—have I got a deal for you!" And while I never bought the property, he *was* always there for me. As my company grew, I could always count on his suggestions and advice.

The nice thing was that as time went by, Art became more and more successful at whatever he did. Once his New York property was sold out, he became a business and marketing consultant, working with some of the biggest companies in the United States. He excelled at teaching and energizing sales forces. He and his wife then started their own company, which specialized in serving the needs of insurance companies. With Art bringing in one major insurance company after another, it was no wonder that his business grew into one of the largest provider service companies in the Northeast.

One night Art and I found ourselves at dinner together, and I asked him if he ever thought of writing a book on selling. I began my spiel, telling him he knows more about sales than anyone I know, and that he's great at it. He looked at me, and without blinking an eye he said, "When do you want the manuscript? Two months, four months? When?" I told him, "Couldn't you at least give me a few minutes to sell you on the idea?" And Art replied, "So you think it was your idea, huh?" That was Art. I really did think it was my idea—really!

What Art delivered was everything I had hoped for. *The Street Smart Sales Pro* is Art Rogen's business Bible, a guide for anyone who has ever dreamed of getting involved in sales. The first half of the book deals with the basics of what anyone needs to have in order to sell: self-confidence. Art explains that the ability to believe in yourself is fundamental to operating any type of business in which you may be involved. The second half of the book provides all the tools necessary to sell any product or service. The many suggestions and advice Art provides in this book can alter the course of any individual's or companies' future for the better. It offers practical intelligence to anyone willing to learn these important elements and tactics. As Art says, you do not have to be a born salesperson to achieve greatness in sales. All that is necessary is that you be willing to do the work required.

I hope the information you find in this book makes a difference in your life. I know that knowing Arthur Rogen has made a difference in mine.

—Rudy Shur
Publisher
Square One Publishers
Garden City Park, New York

Preface

Your first thought might be, "Why did he name this book *The Street Smart Sales Pro*?" Was I trying to be cute, using a clever catch-phrase as a gimmick to get your attention? Yes, the title is meant to catch your attention, but no, it is not meant to be cute. This book is not filled with MBA theories that sound good but don't cut it in the real world of competitive selling. This book was named *The Street Smart Sales Pro* because these are the people who make it happen. They are the achievers and winners in the world of sales. They make the *big bucks;* they are *successful!* If you want a piece of the action and desire to make the most of your selling opportunities, read this book. It is not meant to be gimmicky; or tell you how great you are. This book is meant to provide you with street smart savvy, and if you use it correctly, it will become your sales bible. The knowledge in this book will help lead you to large commissions—and all the perks that go along with it.

I decided to write this book because too often during my thirty years in sales, I have observed sales pros who were not able to see all the wonderful opportunities that their profession could bring them. Many viewed sales as a dead-end job, and became progressively worse sales pros instead of better. The companies that I have consulted with often suffered because of this negative attitude.

This book is written for those who have to communicate the benefits of what they do or represent, which includes just about everyone. Doctors, lawyers, plumbers, gardeners, milkmen, etc., are all selling their services. What do you suppose it means when a person says his doctor has an excellent bedside manner? It means that the doctor has good communication skills and is able to put the patient at ease. In simple terms, he knows how to sell himself. When someone declares that his attorney is the biggest and best in his field, what he is really saying is that his attorney has communicated a sense of optimism, leadership, and trust. He too has sold himself well. After all, from a technical point of view, most of us are not in a position to judge the competency of the people whom we choose to hire. We hope that our judgment is correct; however, we learn about them only after we have interacted with them. *The Street Smart Sales Pro* is therefore designed not only to allow you to open the door to new opportunities, but also to make you the best in whatever you do.

If you are currently in sales, there is a chance that you already know a street smart sales pro. He's the guy who displays that cocky smile when your sales manager announces a sales contest. You see, the street smart sales pro knows the contest is an incentive for the other salespeople to try to increase their sales, whereas it is money in the bank for our street smart sales pro. He knows he's gonna win, and so does everybody else around him. He hasn't lost a contest since he joined the company. Before the first day is over for that contest, our man, the street smart sales pro, has his savings deposit slip filled out. He is such a sure thing; Vegas wouldn't take odds against him. Invariably, he sells any incentive trip he wins, choosing to go to more exotic places—or maybe that was just me.

You might not be aware of it, but you are in the greatest business in the world: sales. Selling does not require you to have a college education or to have been born on the right side of the tracks. It's the great equalizer; it does not discriminate. Many of the street smart sales pros I have known, including yours truly, started out with very little until they were fortunate enough to see the fantastic opportunities a sales career could give them. Street smart sales pros may start out as the underdogs of selling; however, as great as the odds are of their becoming the biggest income producers in their companies, they beat all the odds. In my own case, when I got my first sales job, I saw the opportunity and went for that brass ring. Street smart sales pros don't hide in the corners; they are standouts who bring in the business. If you are not the salesperson you want to be, start your training program now and read this book; gain street smart savvy!

Many underachieving sales pros view street smart sales pros as arrogant con men. If they were con men, they could not produce year after year. What underachievers see as a con is street smart creativity. Street smart sales pros are always looking for new ways of making money. They always see opportunity. For example, if a client's operation is purchased by a larger business, and that customer tells that they have to go with the new company's directives, you can either sit back and kiss the old client good-bye or you can aggressively go after the bigger company, letting your old client help you get your foot in. Get street smart!

Street smart sales pros are rarely in the office. They know where the action is, and it's never at bull sessions at the water cooler. They persevere, they work hard, and they play hard. The harder they play, the more they enjoy their large commissions. Nothing will deter them.

Bugs Bunny is street smart. He doesn't allow anything—not even Elmer Fudd's bullets—to keep him from going after rabbit gold, carrots. Like the street smart rabbit he is, Bugs doesn't quit at the first signs of defeat. He reevaluates and tries again and again if need be.

If you are discouraged and have not accumulated many of the pleasurable items that you want, like a nice home, cars, etc., read this book. Throughout the book is information that will change the way you sell, the way you feel about yourself, and the kinds of goals that you set for yourself. I have written this book so that everyone will be able to benefit from the hundreds of tips and techniques that are offered.

The book is broken down into two parts. The first part deals with the elements of the street smart sales pro. These elements, such as motivation, discipline, and creativity, allow the street smart sales pro to understand what he needs to develop so that he can reach the goals that he has set for himself. The second part of the book presents the skills for the street smart sales pros. In this section, you will be given street smart tools. These tactics will allow you to at least reach the next level of sales success. Many sales pros today simply rely on their personality to sell. That is not enough. To be successful, you have to know how to obtain clients, handle their objections, and close. This book has the tactics that work in your real world of sales. No matter what you sell, these techniques will make you the best at what you do. Get street smart. Don't become an Elmer Fudd salesman, always losing the order to a street smart sales pro.

The best way that you can benefit from this book is to use it. Mark it up; make notes that will help you in your day-to-day selling. This book should become your sales bible. Don't skim through it and deposit it on your book shelf, never to be used again. Reread the chapters that zero in on the skills that you need to work on.

If you're still not convinced to read this book, answer this one question. How often have you walked out of a client's office shaking your head in disbelief and feeling frustrated because you could not close the deal? And I'm sure it has happened with customers whom you know deep down should have been sold. I'll tell you why you didn't make the sale—you haven't developed street smart savvy. If you are tired of coming in second and not making big bucks, take my advice and read this book. Become a street smart sales pro. Underachieving salespeople do not drive expensive cars; street smart sales pros do!

Like lions stalking the plains of Africa, street smart sales pros walk with a confidence that comes about only as a result of enormous success. This book will give you an opportunity to learn the secrets and techniques that make up a street smart sales pro's skills. For the past thirty years, I have used these skills, and they have helped me to buy fantastic luxuries that a poor boy from Brooklyn never believed were within his reach. If you have what it takes to be a street smart sales pro, this book will help you reach for the good things in life. As I said in the opening paragraph, this book is not meant to be cute. This book is based on my experiences as an extremely successful money-making street smart sales pros. Read it; gain the savvy! The only things you have to lose are your preconceived ideas of what it takes to be successful.

Introduction

Street smart sales pros are the people who make things happen. They are the achievers and winners in the world of sales. They make the big bucks; they are successful! Street smart sales pros are confident, cocky, and tough. Nobody is going to take business away from their turf, nobody! Their biggest decision of the year is what color Mercedes they are going to get. Street smart sales pros are heads and shoulders above other salespeople.

Who are these other salespeople? Do these underachievers all sell, look, and talk the same way? Is the world of sales comprised only of super- and underachievers? No, that would be far too simplistic. As a sales trainer for the better part of twenty years, I have found that salespeople fall into four distinct categories. I will give you a description of each. I challenge you to put your ego in your back pocket and give some thought to the kind of salesperson you are, and, more importantly, to the kind of salesperson you want to be. It isn't always easy, but it's street smart.

In addition, I will tell you about the first street smart sales pro I ever met. It was the most exciting and important day of my life. This allowed me to understand that I had the chance to become part of the greatest business in the world of sales. Once you gain the savvy, your opportunities are unlimited.

This book is based on my experiences as an extremely successful money-making street smart sales pro. Let me do for you what that first street smart sales pro did for me thirty-five years ago: make you successful. If you want to earn big commission checks, read this book.

The essence of street smart sales pros is that they hustle and use every skill that they can develop in order to close the sale. If we as sales pros do not write the order during the opportunity that we have with our prospect, you can bet that somebody else will surely follow and take what once was almost ours.

The Four Types of Salespeople

As a sales trainer as well as a consumer, I have been around literally thousands of salespeople and, as a result, have found that they fall into four different classifications.

First, there are the sales pros that I call the *order fakers*. These types of sellers will be able to sell only one out of ten prospects that they talk to. They wear shiny polyester clothing that enables you to see your own reflection as you reject their pleas to purchase. Their product knowledge is poor, their follow-up is nonexistent, and they find the need to talk incessantly about things in which you have absolutely no interest. After being subjected to them for ten or fifteen minutes, you find yourself contemplating a crime that could put you in jail for a very long time! By the way, you can spot these order fakers driving home in Dodge Darts with depressed expressions on their faces. Woody Allen once said, "80 percent of success is showing up." In a sense, even when these order fakers show up, they aren't really there.

I call the second category of sales pros *order takers*. Out of ten potential prospects, they will be able to convert two into actual sales. These people still gravitate to wearing polyester, but at least it's ironed. Scientifically, I don't believe there is a reason for their feet to appear abnormally large. They wear thin-ribbed socks that barely reach their ankles. A dirty brown tint shows on shoes, a result of their never having been polished—a nice touch if they were in construction.

The order takers have reasonably good product knowledge, and as a result should be able to bore you to death with meaningless facts within a fairly short period of time. As in the case of the order fakers, the order takers have to rely on customers who want their product so badly that they overlook their poor sales skills.

The order fakers as well as the order takers rely heavily on low prices in order to close their sales.

Order takers drive Chevys and Fords, and seem to prefer colors such as putrid green and washed-out yellow!

Order makers compose my third classification of sellers. These people sell three out of ten clients. They are reasonably polished and have good product knowledge. They fall short of being charismatic, but to their credit they are not too offensive. They rely heavily on the "once-in-a-life-time" close. This means that if you as a customer decide not to purchase at that very moment, you will never again be able to take advantage of that "once-in-a-lifetime" opportunity that they are proposing.

Their appearance is neat, colors of their clothes generally do not clash, and for the most part they look fairly professional. When they are feeling good about themselves, they have a tendency to wear every piece of jewelry that they own. Some develop "aurous syndrome," which is curvature of the neck caused by the excessive weight of their gold chains. They try to engage clients in conversation in order to discover customer needs; unfortunately, their approach is about as subtle as that of Vince Vaughn in any of his movie roles.

A showy red Chrysler 300 appears to be their preference in cars; probably because it looks like a Bentley—a car they know they will never be able to afford. They order all sorts of extra gizmos that not only inform them of who is in the car next to them, but, in addition, the number of times their kids are going to ask, "Are we there yet?" The car seats are covered in velour. Order makers rationalize that velour is superior to leather since it does not get hot in the summer. Deep down they know this is sour grapes, especially when they have the arduous task of cleaning up after one of their kids becomes car sick!

Order shakers round out our last category of salespeople. These shakers are the cream of the crop; they are street smart sales pros. They use their savvy to make big bucks. The street smart shakers are selfish; they do not like to share their customers with anybody. They want it all, and, for the most part, get it. Fakers, takers, and makers, like vultures scavenging through a carcass devoured by a hungry lion, pick up only bits and pieces of business left behind by the street smart sales pros. They buy the cars they set their sights on, and like the dream cars they drive, these shakers are sleek, silky smooth, and fast on their feet. They understand that people buy for their own reasons, not the seller's; thus, they are able to maximize every sales situation that they encounter. Most superstar sales pros fall into this classification. I say most because there are situations in which a faker, taker, or maker happens to be in the right place at the right time, enabling him to get that one contract that affords him success far beyond his abilities. It's like knowing that eventually someone will win the lottery. The thing is, it most likely will not be you—so hoping for lightning to strike is not a substitute for preparation.

The shakers can be extremely charming, and are able to present themselves in a fascinating and electrifying manner. They are not afraid to be different or outrageous. They are constantly searching for new ways to improve themselves. They do not fear competition; they welcome it. They do not sell prices; they sell themselves. They are confident that they will survive and achieve greatness; they are street smart!

There is no question that I used a stretch of the imagination to embellish the negative characteristics of the faker, taker, and maker. What I did not exaggerate is the startling fact that most sellers engaged in selling cannot sell. Neither did I exaggerate that the street smart sales pros are the achievers of the world.

Who Are You?

I ask you at this point: What kind of salesperson do you want to be? Only you can answer this question. Fakers, takers, and makers have sold only one person well—themselves! They have sold themselves on the fact that they have done their very best to be where they are. Some might say that they could have done better if they had just gotten a few breaks; but they didn't, and this is the way it has to be. Shakers, who are street smart sales pros, also sold themselves well—the difference being that they sold themselves on the fact that success is within their reach and that they control their own destiny. They know that being rich is definitely a whole lot better than being poor.

Years ago, I decided not to settle for mediocrity. Settling is for losers, and I wanted no part of that. I was determined to be a winner. Let me tell you a little about myself and how I was persuaded never to accept second place.

Before I started my career in selling, a friend convinced me to attend a recruiting seminar for a company called United States Properties. They were looking for salespeople, and as part of their program they retained the services of Larry Wilson, future author of *One Minute Salesperson*, to speak on the advantages of entering the profession of sales. At the time, I was an elementary school teacher, clinging to the security of the position with rather low aspirations for myself. As Wilson strutted across the stage, I was immediately impressed with the confidence that emanated from him. Within seconds, he had all the people in the audience listening to his words as if he were a prophet—and in my case he was, for at that moment I was about to become a convert. I wanted more, and Larry Wilson convinced me that I could achieve it through the sales profession. I became a believer!

What impressed me most about Wilson's speech that day was his description of a salesman. Before I heard him speak, I thought all salesmen were like Willy Loman, the title character of Arthur Miller's play *Death of a Salesman*—some poor soul carrying a large beat-up sample case, desperately trying to convince someone to purchase his wares in order to make ends meet for the week. This was far from an accurate description, according to Larry Wilson. For Wilson, a professional salesperson was an individual who had the opportunity to earn literally as much as he wanted. In addition, if he acquired the skills needed to become a professional salesperson, he would not only gain riches, but also have more security in his job than in any other occupation, since, as he put it, companies could not exist unless they employed salespeople who were able to sell their products or services. Though I had never thought of selling in that vein, I knew it had to be true. Logically, no matter how well a company manufactured a product or performed a service, if that company could not get the word out and get someone to say, "Yes, I would like one," the company could not survive.

Three hours or so later, I was determined to give up my teaching position and enter the sales training program offered by United States Properties. After filling out the application, I practically ran home to tell my wife, Sally, about my good fortune. The moment I arrived and began informing my wife about my career decision, my selling profession began. You see, my wife had not heard Larry Wilson speak. She did not believe I would have more security working as a commission salesman than an elementary school teacher, even though I was then making only enough to pay our essential bills. To make matters worse, just as I was about to convince my wife of the merits of my new venture, my parents dropped by our apartment. Upon hearing about my new career, my mother spoke to me as if I were about to commit the most heinous of acts, killing the two of them. My mother cried that if her college-educated son left teaching, he would surely be murdering his father and her. My father took a more rational approach. He hoped that I had temporary insanity, and was sure I would regain my senses in the morning, especially after I realized how much money and sacrifice it had taken them to send me to college. I knew at that moment that if I were able to overcome the objections of the three of them, I had the makings to be the world's greatest salesman.

To be perfectly honest, I was able to convince only my wife that this was the right thing for me to do. My parents would not listen to anything I said, and again threatened to put their heads in the oven if I indeed left teaching. In addition, they informed me that if they survived the oven and I came to them for any sort of financial support, it would not be available. With all this encouragement, I resigned from my teaching position that very week.

Looking back, it was the best decision I ever made. I became a salesman for United States Properties, rising from an entry-level position to that of vice president of marketing for their Eastern Marine Division in four years. My life was never the same. Within two years, I became their top in-home sales rep, earning enough money to buy a magnificent home on the north shore of Long Island, thirty miles outside of New York City. Three years later I made their prestigious "Million Dollar Club" and, as a result, the company held a dinner in my honor for 300-plus guests. I got to invite my mom and dad as well— to prove to them that the money wasn't coming from my secret career as a bank robber.

I left United States Properties three years later in order to start my own real estate development company. Six highly successful years later

I sold my interests so that I could concentrate on my first love, teaching. Not teaching elementary school, but teaching salespeople who wanted to become successful in the greatest of all professions, sales. And for fifteen years, that's exactly what I did. I instructed salespeople on how to take advantage of all the wonderful opportunities that are out there in sales. I have accomplished this by developing my own sales consulting firm. Over the years, I worked with all types of industries, big and small, corporations, and independently owned businesses. What they have in common is a need to maximize their sales opportunities, and that is exactly what my programs and seminars provided—a way to turn their average salespeople into street smart sales pros.

What this boils down to is that these street smart sales pros have taken the principles of sales to a level much higher than most people engaged in selling are aware of. I have studied these principles for decades and, more importantly, have put them into practical use, enabling me to close many an important deal.

My Goal

This book is specifically designed to give you both the understanding and the skills it takes to become street smart. I've divided this book into two parts: first, elements of the street smart sales pro, such as motivation, discipline, and creativity; and second, the meat-and-potato sales tactics used by street smart sales pros.

Whether you come from the Back Bay of Boston, the foothills of Tennessee, or the desert towns of New Mexico is not important. All I know is that businesses are always looking for sales reps who stand out—salespeople who can help them grow and prosper, and who, in turn, can reap the rewards of their companies' prosperity. Knowledge is power, and I have put the knowledge I have accumulated over many years in this book to help you become a street smart sales pro, a winner! All you have to do is read—practice what you read—and then go for it! You'll find it's definitely worth the effort.

PART 1

Elements of the Street Smart Sales Pro

1

The Toys

I like nice things. I like good cars, comfortable homes, great vacations, and the freedom not to worry about bills! This statement may sound arrogant, but the truth of the matter is that in many instances money is the motivating factor for the street smart sales pro. Of course there are other variables, but the key point is that these extremely successful sales pros must be motivated by something. They know what they want, and they are motivated to achieve because of the goals that they set for themselves. Street smart sales pros do not get up in the morning dreading to go to work. In fact, they cannot wait till the next day arrives, simply because they know it gives them another opportunity to get closer to their goals.

As a boy growing up with my parents and two sisters in a one-bedroom apartment located in a poor melting-pot section of Brooklyn, New York, I used to dream about how fantastic it would be to have some of the luxuries I saw in the movies, like large homes, fancy cars, and snazzy clothes. Being only eight years old, I probably would have considered it a luxury to have my own bedroom and not have to sleep on an old high-riser couch with my sister Linda, who constantly twisted and turned in her sleep and eventually stole all the blanket. One dreadful night, she accidentally flipped up the bar that lowered the bed, nearly decapitating me. Whoever said those were the good old days had to be rich! No way did he share his bed or stand on line to go to the bathroom in the morning.

Even as an eight-year-old boy, I was determined to succeed. My goal was to become rich enough to buy my mother a nice house where she would be able to garden all day. I had no idea back then that all my dreams would come true once I developed my street smart skills.

You are never too young or old to start setting goals for yourself. Some people, like myself, start as young children dreaming about the good things in life. Others, like my uncle Mickey, begin a second career in their late sixties. The key point is that people who achieve and live full and exciting lives are constantly setting goals for themselves, no matter their ages. I guarantee that if you don't have goals motivating you to take action, you most likely are an underachiever, sleepwalking through life.

In this chapter, we will examine how the street smart sales pro uses goals to help him reach greatness. Read this chapter, giving it great thought. It will help you develop and understand the proper way of establishing goals. And don't worry if some of your goals sound shallow or superficial. Once you're rich, you can always reevaluate.

Set Goals

All of us talk about goals in some fashion. Many would like to earn more money, drive a nicer car, have a larger home, etc. Unfortunately, most people merely talk about their goals, instead of working and planning to obtain them. This holds true especially in the selling profession. We set quotas and commissions that we would like to earn, yet few of us make a conscious effort to work at these goals to achieve success. At times, goals are not even our own, but are set by others, making them even more meaningless. A sales manager often demands a certain amount of business, but in many cases this is a minimum standard that enables him to keep his job. In plain English, even if the sales manager is not aware of it, he is reinforcing the notion that mediocrity is satisfactory.

There is nothing mediocre about street smart sales pros. These clever sales pros are not afraid of setting high standards for themselves. Street smart sales pros do not sell themselves short, settling for second best. They are not content just to go along meeting company sales quotas, which offer little more than job security. Street smart sales pros are always looking to increase their sales from one month to the next. The goals that the street smart sales pros set for themselves are considerably higher than any quotas that their company can possibly establish for them.

While I was a real estate salesman at United States Properties, some of my fellow salespeople used to question me as to why I pushed myself so hard. When I disclosed to them that my goal for the year was to make fifty-two sales—amounting to my selling a property each and every week—they thought I was absolutely crazy. In fact, some said that even if I somehow managed to accomplish this sales feat, I would surely pay the price by burning myself out. The company quota at the time was twenty sales a year.

I am happy to report that having met my own sales quota for the year, I did not come close to burning myself out. What was the price I paid for setting higher standards for myself? By the end of the year, I was able to buy a beautiful house, a great car, and provide for my family's needs—something that I never could have accomplished on my old teacher's salary. Many of my colleagues who questioned my sanity became burnt out and disillusioned, leaving the field for what they believed to be greener pastures. If only they had set higher standards for themselves, they might have been able to take advantage of the opportunities that were right in front of them, and become neighbors of mine!

Ready, Set, Prepare

The street smart sales pro realizes that only through hard work and preparation can he expect to reach the high standards that he sets for himself. Because the sales rep is so good at what he does, people do not believe that he works or prepares as hard as he does. They think that large commission checks come to the street smart sales pro as if they were acts of God. This is nonsense. Street smart sales pros work very hard. They know that if they do not prepare well they are wasting valuable opportunities for themselves.

Dr. Robert Schuller, author of *Move Ahead With Possibility Thinking,* states that "spectacular achievement is always preceded by unspectacular preparation." You've got to love that. It's so simple and yet so true.

Preparation can be boring, mundane, and repetitive, but the street smart sales pro is aware that there is no substitute for it. The wise sales pro is always looking to learn more about his product, his service, or his client. He wants to be prepared to answer any questions that might come up. And just as important, he promotes new ways that the features of his product or service can best meet the needs of his client.

The street smart sales pro frequently rehearses his presentation, seeing if there are any additional ways to fine-tune it. He knows that only through hard work, preparation, and scrutiny will he be able to remain on top of his presentation, sounding knowledgeable, fresh, and enthusiastic.

On many occasions, salespeople will approach me and ask, "Arthur, why do you work so hard?" My reply to that question is always the same. I describe how one day, while walking through the streets of New York City, I came across a parked car that had a bumper sticker that read, "THE ONE WHO ACCUMULATES THE MOST TOYS BEFORE HE DIES WINS!" I thought for a moment, and decided that here was one game that I absolutely had to win. It is a game that I take very seriously and work extremely hard at. Once I had begun to accumulate some of my "toys," I discovered that my desire to prepare, work, and win became stronger and stronger.

Most of us want the toys, but when push comes to shove, are not willing to put the effort into obtaining them. Fakers and takers sell themselves on the idea that they are working hard simply because they arrive at the office in the morning and leave in the evening. Fakers and takers, in many cases, do put in long hours, but they are nonproductive hours. Some even enjoy hanging out in the office. These sales pros are about as productive as the chairs that they sit on. Others convince themselves that they have found a shortcut to success. Sadly for them, they realize too late in their careers that this is never the case.

The story I am about to tell you is absolutely true and will further illustrate my point about how salespeople can easily fool themselves into believing that they are working as hard as they should.

When I was first married, my wife and I lived in an apartment house. Our next-door neighbor was a sunglass salesman named Steve. Whenever I happened to meet Steve in the building, he was either off to the golf course, tennis courts, or whatever other recreation he could find. I could never recall seeing him dressed for work. After a while, I questioned Steve about his work hours. Steve smiled and indicated that he had the perfect job. He told me how he did most of his business on the telephone, avoiding the inconvenience of making outside sales visits to his clients. He indicated that he had little difficulty making his sales quotas and was quite proud of the fact that he was able to fool his sales manager regarding how hard he was working. About five years ago, my wife and I ran into Steve and his wife at Macy's, a New York department store. Naturally, we asked each other how things were and what kind of work we were doing. Things had not changed much for Steve. He was still selling sunglasses and living in the same small apartment. He stated that he did not get the breaks over the years, declaring that all the promotions were going to the younger guys who kissed up to their managers.

There are a million Steves out there, fooling the boss, wishing and hoping for success, but not willing to put in the hard work or preparation needed to achieve it.

If you want to become a street smart sales pro earning the big bucks, you must work hard and study your profession constantly. Because most sellers choose not to work hard, you have an opportunity to give yourself a major advantage. Of course, if you want success without hard work and preparation, you could always try and win the lottery or wait for an inheritance, but for most of us, this is not a reality. Abraham Lincoln said, "If I had nine hours to cut down a tree, I would spend six hours sharpening my axe." If you want to become street smart, start sharpening your axe. There are no shortcuts. Without preparation and hard work, success will surely not follow.

Write It, Read It, Believe It

Street smart sales pros write down their goals. Not only do they write down their goals, they write down how these goals will benefit them. The street smart sales pro is keenly aware that this is the only way that his goals will become meaningful to him. In a sense, the street smart sales pro has made a contract for success with himself, a contract he surely would not want to break.

The exercise of writing out his goals reinforces for the street smart sales pro all the benefits that he will achieve once her goals have been met. This way, if he becomes discouraged, unmotivated, or sidetracked along the way, the street smart sales pro can pull out his contract and clearly see the rewards that he will receive if he perseveres.

A few years ago I wanted to buy this classic Corvette sports car that I saw at the local dealership. I remember being a teenager, working as a caddy, and envying the people whom I saw driving these cars. The color that I liked best was racing green, which happened to be the exact color that this dealership had. The car was definitely not very practical for a family of five, but was, nevertheless, a toy that I really wanted to have. I rationalized that if I could increase my sales by four a month, I could buy the car within a four month period of time, without spending money that had been earmarked for other family projects.

I knew this would not be an easy task, and would require that I work even longer and harder. I also knew that there would be times when I would lose some motivation, especially when I would have to refuse my friends' invitations to play golf or tennis. But I wanted my dream car. To insure that I would sustain my motivation, I wrote down my goal. Below is an example of how I typically write out my goals:

Goal. During the months of June, July, and August, my goal is to increase my sales by three a month.

Benefits. These additional sales will allow me to purchase that racing green color Corvette convertible that I saw at Competition Motors. Stay motivated and enthusiastic. Remember, you already put a deposit down!

To be perfectly honest, I had to pull out my contract more than a few times that summer, especially when I was working while my friends were playing. But by the end of July, a month ahead of schedule, I accomplished my goal. I felt like a teenager as I motored around in my racing green-colored Corvette!

Underachievers, like the fakers, takers, and makers, never put down their goals in writing. If they did, they would discover that they are constantly breaking their own contracts. Because they do not write down their goals, the benefits of their goals become less important to them as they experience difficulty. As a result of this, there is no way that the fakers, takers, and makers are able to sustain their motivation over a long period of time. This is one of the reasons that they never achieve success—they frequently change their goals when they see the first signs of defeat.

Become successful—write down your goals. Like the street smart sales pro, become accountable to yourself.

Define Your Goals

In addition to writing down his goals, the street smart sales pro is aware that a key element to his success is to have specific and well-defined goals. In the goal that I described in the preceding paragraphs, I wrote down the specific color, racing green, as well as the specific model car, Corvette, that I wanted to buy, not being content to merely list "car" as my goal.

The street smart sales pro's goals are so real and specific that he can clearly imagine he is in possession of them. For example, if a sales pro's goal is to own a sports car or boat, he is able to visualize his hair blowing in the wind as he goes speeding down the highway in his red Porsche convertible or sailing on the open ocean air in a Chris-Craft yacht, cutting through the pounding waves. Notice that I didn't just say a car or a boat without naming the specific types. Street smart sales pros know specifically what they want. They want that red Porsche, they want that Chris-Craft yacht that sleeps eight. They don't just list as a goal a car or a boat.

If a street smart sales pro's goal is to earn a lot of money, he will write down the specific sum that he wants to earn. If your goals are not specific and well-defined, you will not be able to fully appreciate how they will benefit you once you achieve them. As a result, you will have trouble sustaining your motivation if things do not go as smoothly as you would like. Because of this, fakers, takers, and makers are like boats without sails, drifting from one goal to another, missing out on the success that they had hoped to achieve.

Define your goals so you can see vividly how they will benefit you. Set your sails and begin to steer your ship on the course of success!

Avoid Conflicting Goals

Street smart sales pros do not have conflicting goals. Referring back to my goal of buying that Corvette, it would have been impossible for me to have set the goals as both increasing my sales production and simultaneously cutting my working hours in half in order to pursue other interests.

People who have conflicting goals set themselves up for failure. It is not possible to eat junk food all day and lose weight at the same time. When you are writing down your goals, make sure that they are not in conflict with each other. If they are, reevaluate them and choose the one that will offer you the most benefits.

Make Your Goals Achievable

Street smart sales pros set goals that are believable to them. They have the confidence that they can obtain these objectives. Underachievers become frustrated and discouraged in many cases because their goals are not goals, but are merely unrealistic wishes. Deep down, the under-achiever really does not believe he is capable of reaching these goals. These unsustainable goals only keep him frozen in place. Instead of taking appropriate action, he hopes for a miracle to occur.

For example, I love to play golf, but it would be a totally unreal-istic goal for me to set my sights on scoring in the seventies, even if Tiger Woods helped me putt. If I persisted in this unrealistic goal, I would soon become frustrated and lose the love for the game that I cherish so dearly.

Don't be a dreamer. Set goals that are realistic and believable to you. Be proactive; become street smart.

Set Time Frames

Street smart sales pros always set a time frame for their goals that is not so far in the future that the goals become meaningless. Providing too little time to accomplish a goal will also end in frustration. Giving our-selves too much time does not allow us to sharpen our skills. I recom-mend ninety-day goals. That does not mean we cannot plan for the entire year. What I am saying is, we should have check points every ninety days to see if we are on target and, if not, we should make the necessary adjustments to get back on track.

Make sure to ask questions of other sellers about how long a typical sale takes. Setting timeframes should always be based on past experience. Once we have a clearer idea of how long a goal should take to achieve, we can always try to raise the bar and improve that time period.

Keep It Simple

Be careful not to set up too many goals. This too can set you up for failure, frustration, and procrastination. Fakers, takers, and makers have loads of goals. They want to be rich, they want to be thin, they want, they want, they want . . . They have so many wants that they lose sight of their priorities. In addition, once one goal becomes a little difficult to achieve, they have a tendency to move to another objective that they believe is more obtainable. In the end, very little will be accomplished.

Making It Happen

How do you reach your goals once they are set? First of all, like the street smart sales pro, you must make a daily commitment to work as hard as you can. Also, it is important to keep a positive attitude. Street smart sales pros think of themselves as winners.

At times, no matter how diligently you work, you will not always succeed in reaching your goals. The sensible street smart sales pro understands that this is part of life, not just in sales, and tries to maintain a positive attitude towards himself as well as his work. The street smart sales pro is aware that even though he did not reach an original objective, he can still have a positive learning experience. In his book *Seven Seconds to Success in Selling,* Willie Gayle quotes Tryon Edwards, "Some of the best lessons we ever learn, we learn from our mistakes and failures. The error of the past is the wisdom and success of the future."

The street smart sales pro makes it a habit to stay away from negative thoughts and from people who will discourage him from reaching his goals. Later on in the book I will discuss in greater detail the importance of having a positive attitude, as well as the negative effects that people can have on us.

Street smart sales pros know that in order to reach their goals they have to have excellent time management. They know that there are 86,400 seconds in a day, each one precious. Once they have passed, they can never be recaptured. Underachievers do not use their time wisely. Don't pretend that you are working when you are not. If you are behind your desk thinking about a round of golf, go play, but plan on how you are going to make up the time. If your mind is not on your work, utilize it on recreation, as long as it doesn't constantly take over your daily routine. Productive recreation can produce better results than nonproductive staring out the window.

Lastly, make things happen; do not wait and hope for good things to happen. George Bernard Shaw said, "The people who get on in this world are the people who get up and look for the circumstances they want, and, if they can't find them, make them." Street smart sales pros act quickly on their ideas and take advantage of opportunities when they present themselves. If your goals are written and believable, you can take hold of your life and make it happen.

Consider This

It's easy to read about other people setting goals, but it's a lot harder to see exactly where you yourself stand in relationship to what you really want. The following seventeen questions are designed to help you come face to face with your desire to succeed as a sales pro. Read these questions one at a time, think about them carefully, and answer them on a sheet of paper. And if you can't find the time or a pencil and pad to write down your answers, I suggest you skip down to the next paragraph.

1. Is your career going as planned?

2. What single factor has held you back from achieving more?

3. Do you see yourself as a winner?

4. If not, why not?

5. Do you set high standards for yourself?

6. If not, why not?

7. Are you working as hard as you can in your present job?

8. If not, why not?

9. Do you find your job boring?

10. Do you consider being a sales pro a rewarding profession?

11. If you were given an opportunity to enter another field, would you choose to do so?

12. List the goals that you would like to obtain during the next twelve months.

13. List all the obstacles that you believe you will encounter before you will be able to reach your goals.

14. List all the benefits that you will receive once these goals are met.

15. Do you see enough benefits coming to you to encourage your putting in the effort to reach these goals?

16. Write down a date when you will commit to making your goals a reality.

17. Lastly, can you visualize having in your possession that first toy that you will buy yourself once you begin to achieve success?

For some of you, this can be a very revealing questionnaire to answer. The truth is that some people just aren't cut out to be sellers. If you can't fill in the answers to the questions above, or the answers you have aren't making sense to you, maybe selling isn't for you. There is absolutely no shame in recognizing the fact that the type of success I am talking about is not going to make you happy. Making money is not always a prime motivation. On the other hand, if your answers are in line with what you've just read in this chapter, you've just taken the first step towards becoming a street smart sales pro!

2

The Fire

A fire burns way, way down inside the belly of the street smart sales pro, giving her the motivation to achieve. When she goes out to see a client she is self-assured, prepared, and primed to connect with this client. The street smart sales pro uses this approach in order to achieve the high standards that she sets for herself. She is relentless; her fire keeps her working at a high, enthusiastic level, even during difficult times. This separates the street smart sales pro from the fakers, takers, and makers, whose fire is quickly extinguished as they experience problems that send them packing to the world of the non-achiever.

If you want the same type of fire that burns in the street smart sales pro, you have to have certain elements in place. These elements are the things that fuel the fire. You not only have to understand them, but also trust and believe in them; only then will you be on your way to becoming a street smart sales pro.

The Force That Moves Mountains

What is motivation? Psychologists tell us it is an incentive for an individual to take action in some manner or form. Even though psychologists cannot agree on the mechanics of motivation, they do agree on the fact that each individual has particular needs. As soon as one need is satisfied, another need appears and motivates the individual to respond. Shelter, food, security (in the form of money), and recognition are some of the common needs that most people possess.

Street smart sales pros share these common needs; the only difference is that because of their standards and aspirations, the needs they have are at a much higher level. For example, someone may find that earning $100 thousand a year will satisfy her need for security, whereas the street smart sales pro who has greater ambitions and wants would not feel secure unless she made $500 thousand a year or more.

Everybody who has to work does so to satisfy the basic need of shelter: keeping a roof overhead. Many people, like the fakers, takers, and makers, would be happy enough living in small apartments or houses so far from their jobs that they would have to spend half their lives commuting. Street smart sales pros are also motivated to satisfy the basic need of shelter, although their idea of shelter may be a mansion!

A few years ago I had a consulting assignment with a company that manufactured stationery supplies. The owner of the company was in a quandary as to whether he should fire one of his salespeople. He explained that this salesman had an excellent appearance, was articulate, and seemed to have all the ability in the world, yet in the last two years was never more than a marginal producer for the company. The owner wanted me to see if I could determine why he performed so poorly.

After interviewing the salesman, it was easy to discover just what the problem was: He had little motivation to move ahead. The salesman told me he was living with his wife in the bottom apartment of a two-family house owned by his in-laws—*rent free!* Being mechanically inclined, he was proud of the fact that he was able to keep his 2006 Honda going with 150 thousand miles on it. *No car payment!* On top of this, he described his mother-in-law as the world's greatest cook, whose skills he took advantage of at every meal. *No food bills!*

It is no wonder that this sales pro did not perform; he had no incentives! Everybody was taking care of him. His aspirations were low and he had no difficulty meeting his needs. He was the original Freddie Freeloader! I must be honest; this is more than enough to give a father like myself nightmares, since I have two daughters of my own. Even though on the surface, this sales pro appeared to exhibit all the traits necessary for becoming a superstar, he lacked one important ingredient: motivation to succeed.

Yes, You Can

Street smart sales pros keep their motivation levels high by having a positive attitude. This positive attitude turns them into fine-tuned fighting machines, defeating any obstacles that get in the way. Their language is positive; they use phrases such as, "Nothing can keep me from achieving success" and "I will reach my goals." When a street smart sales pro goes on a sales call, she can vividly picture herself making a sale. She sees herself effectively handling any objections that might come up. She sees herself getting the signed contract. Never does she see herself failing; street smart sales pros are always positive.

Underachievers of the world carry a negative attitude around as if it were part of their anatomy. They use language like, "I'm not sure I can do that" and "How can they expect us to reach that sales goal?" As a result of this negative attitude, they can never visualize themselves as winners.

Street smart sales pros, not wanting to be negatively influenced by others, choose to stay away from people who do not have a positive attitude. They are aware that negative people have an almost subliminal effect on those around them. When a new incentive is announced, all the sales pros are at first excited and motivated to achieve. By the second week, one-third of the sales pros start to become negative. During the third week, these negative spreaders of doubt become a negative influence on the next third of the sales force. Before the month is up, only the street smart sales pros, who choose to stay away from these negative people as if they had the plague, remain motivated to reach their goals.

It's a fact that you cannot tailor-make the circumstances in your life, but you can tailor-make the attitudes to fit those circumstances before they arise. Street smart sales pros do this by always trying to remain positive. The street smart sales pro will not allow negative people to eat away at her motivation as if she were a log infested with termites!

Street smart sales pros understand that identifying a problem is the first step toward discovering a solution. They know that the key to their success is to be solution-oriented and not problem-oriented. They are the eternal optimists in the sales profession. As a result of their positive and optimistic attitude, street smart sales pros see opportunity where others see doom and gloom. Problems are viewed as challenges that street smart sales pros work like the devil to overcome.

In the 1970s, when I was first starting out in real estate, America went through a major gas crisis. People had to wait on long lines, hoping to get enough gas to get them through the week—much like the gas lines that appeared during the aftermath of Hurricane Sandy in the Northeast. Tempers flared and fights broke out on a number of these gas station lines.

Needless to say, it was not the best of times to be selling recreational property to New Yorkers, ninety miles from their homes. The majority of my fellow sales reps virtually gave up trying to sell property. I viewed this as a challenge. There was no way that I would allow the gas shortage to keep me from making the living that I had become accustomed to.

Through hard and persuasive work, I was able to line up a few gas station owners who were willing to provide my customers with enough gas to get them up to see my property. At the time, I made arrangements to pay the owners fifty dollars for every one of my clients that they gave gas to. This was a small price to pay, especially when you consider that I would make several thousand in a single commission.

If the customer bought the property, I gave her a card indicating that she was a member of the community upstate. As a result, she was able to get gas by paying the owner a five dollar premium when she filled up. My customers were tickled pink. In some cases, I'm not so sure that they didn't just buy the property in order to get gas. Since the development had its own gas pumps, customers had no trouble going home.

As a result of my identifying a problem, and at the same time keeping a positive attitude, I was able to come up with a solution that turned a possible disaster into a money-making benefit to myself. It was not too long before the company observed my gas plan and made arrangements for the other sales reps' clients to get gas. I made additional thousands by winning every sales incentive that the company offered during the gas crisis.

Become street smart—recognize all the fabulous opportunities that surround you. During World War II, Winston Churchill implored the

English people not to lose heart as a result of the merciless blitz the German air force had launched against England. He told his people that "a pessimist sees the difficulty in every opportunity; an optimist sees the opportunity in every difficulty." Take Churchill's advice and become street smart!

Street smart sales pros keep their motivation high by not allowing failure to affect them.

Fearing Fear

Many sales pros, like the fakers, takers, and makers, fear failing so badly that it totally extinguishes their fire, causing them to abandon their efforts to achieve. They get depressed and begin to feel sorry for themselves. They say things such as, "I can't catch a break," "I knew I shouldn't have tried that," and "Things never go right for me."

Because sales pros are so afraid to fail, they play it safe. Their motivation is so low that they only go after accounts that they feel secure in selling, in many cases avoiding the ones that offer the greatest monetary rewards. Street smart sales pros do not look for the easy way out. They are motivated to go where the money is, no matter how difficult it can get. The street smart sales pros will stop trying to sell these accounts only when they get a "yes."

My father had a friend named Henry who was a children's clothing salesman. Henry traveled throughout the northern part of New York. He was a hard-working salesman who frequently traveled hundreds of miles a day. Unfortunately, because Henry had a fear of failing, he worked harder and not smarter. Henry used to tell my dad and me how he needed the patience of a saint when working with small mom-and-pop shops, constantly waiting for the owner to finish with a customer in order to show his samples.

When I questioned Henry as to why he would continue to sell only these small types of accounts, he mumbled that he didn't have the connections to get the bigger buyers to see his line. I knew this was bull. Fear of failure kept Henry from becoming a top producer. Henry took the route that made him feel the most secure—small mom-and-pop stores where he wasn't intimidated. He was so afraid that he was not able to motivate himself to go after the real money-making accounts, preferring to continue to work harder for smaller commissions.

Embracing Fear

Street smart sales pros understand that the only way to avoid failure is to try, and so street smart sales pros never give up trying. Street smart sales pros are so motivated that they never see failure as failure, but only as a learning experience. If they fail to reach their objective, street smart sales pros learn from their mistakes, and if anything, are more motivated to try again. Thomas Edison, in response to a question regarding the enormous amount of failure that he encountered while conducting his experiments, replied, "I did not fail a thousand times; I learned a thousand ways that wouldn't work." Street smart sales pros are so motivated that they do not base their success on the number of times they have failed, but on the number of times that they have succeeded.

If a street smart sales pro finds that she has a weakness, she works hard to overcome it, realizing that it is vital to her success in life and work that she recognize her own weaknesses and limitations. The street smart sales pro is comfortable admitting that she has a problem; she doesn't bury her head in the sand or blame others for her shortcomings. Most nonachievers choose to run away from their flaws, lacking the strength to try to overcome them.

When I first started out in sales, I was not very good at prospecting on the telephone. I found it boring and did not particularly enjoy being hung up on all day. Instead of running away from my problem, I decided to write out different telephone scripts, practicing on my wife, Sally, every night after work. In the beginning, I was so bad that she'd hang up on me. My own wife, for God's sake! Nevertheless, I practiced like I was trying to get a part in a Broadway play. Nobody was going to stop me from getting that role. I was motivated to succeed. I was going to become the best telephone solicitor I could be, never having to depend on others to supply me with leads.

Examine your strengths and weaknesses as a salesperson. If you are to become street smart, you will have to work to overcome any deficiencies you might have.

There Is No Shame In Success

The desire for recognition helps keep the fire burning in the street smart sales pro. She wants to be recognized for her good work by her fellow workers as well as by her family and friends. She rewards her own good work by purchasing luxury cars, expensive clothes, etc.

The first time I started making real money, I bought a fabulous midnight-blue Cadillac. The seats had the softest leather I have ever felt. Every conceivable gadget was elaborately spread across the dashboard. For me, at that point in my life, owning a Cadillac meant that I had arrived!

I drove that Cadillac up and down and around my neighborhood, hoping that my neighbors would see me behind the wheel. At the time, I was doing quite well in business, and I guess my ego wanted everybody to see just how well I was actually doing.

When I first showed the car to my dad, he looked at me with eyes welling with tears and said, "Arthur, my big-shot son, I'm proud of you." Those words meant an awful lot to me. To some folks that may seem shallow, but it is the truth. The recognition that I receive from my family, friends, and peers helps to give me the motivation needed to acquire additional material comforts associated with success. In the same way, when you've earned the opportunity to stand out among your peers, you have no reason to hide the fact. Success begets success.

Consider This

In summary, the needs of street smart sales pros are no different than the needs of those who do not achieve great success. Both types want security, shelter, and recognition. The difference between winners and losers is the level of motivation. The motivation of street smart sales pros to achieve is stronger. Street smart sales pros, because of their high motivation, are not afraid to fail, and will create new challenges for themselves and go after the difficult sales. They do not blame others for their own mistakes or weaknesses. Their motivation is such that they set high standards for themselves and fully expect to reach them, no matter what it takes. They derive enormous gratification from the recognition that they receive from their peers.

The following questions are designed to help you look in the mirror and see exactly how brightly your own fire burns. Read these ten questions, think about them carefully, and answer them on a sheet of paper.

1. Do you have a specific well-defined goal that will motivate you to take immediate action?

2. If not, why not?

3. Do you generally have a positive attitude in relation to your work?

4. If not, why not?

5. Are the people around you—your wife, boss, friends, and fellow workers—positive or negative?

6. When something doesn't work out in your plans, what is your immediate reaction? What is your long-term reaction?

7. Do you avoid taking action on your ideas because you have a fear of failure?

8. What motivates you most: money, recognition, or security?

9. Where do you actually stand in relation to your own motivation?

10. If you are not where you would like to be, why aren't you?

At this point, if you are still not motivated enough to continue reading, selling is probably not for you. However, if your answers are in line with what you've just read in this chapter, you've taken the second step towards becoming a street smart sales pro!

3

Keeping It Up

If the people who make *Call of Duty* had a sales video game that required the same Herculean effort to win, they would be wise to name it *The Street Smart Sales Pro—Sales Warrior!* For the street smart sales pro is the ultimate fighter, constantly battling enemies such as rejection, frustration, objection, and discouragement in order to come out on top and win the war of the big bucks!

If you are not a successful sales soldier of fortune, you must learn how to develop the single most important element of the successful street smart sales pro, which is perseverance. The ability to persevere during the most trying times is the driving force that allows the street smart sales pro to remain focused on what he wants to achieve. If I sound like a martial arts instructor, good! For only with that quality of persistence will you be on your way to becoming a street smart sales pro.

Stay the Course

Most people confuse perseverance with motivation. These concepts are not the same. They are worlds apart. The majority of underachievers can be very motivated, but still fall far short of their goals. Under-achievers lack the ability to keep going when they see the first signs of defeat, and so can never reach their objectives, no matter how bright or creative they happen to be.

President Calvin Coolidge once said, "Press on: Nothing in the world can take the place of perseverance. Talent will not; nothing is more common than unsuccessful men with talent. Genius will not; the world is full of educated derelicts. Persistence and determination are omnipotent." This from a man nicknamed "Silent Cal." Although he may have been a man of few words, his perseverance paid off big time, getting him to the highest position in the country. Just like Cal, street smart sales pros have the ability to press on.

Typically, the underachiever's initial enthusiasm gives him the motivation to take action, but disappears as he experiences the first signs of difficulty. Unlike the fakers, takers, and makers, the street smart sales pro has a fifth gear that kicks in once his initial enthusiasm leaves, an extra store of energy that gives him the necessary persever- ance to reach his goals.

Throughout my career as a sales trainer, I have come across many, many supposedly motivated salespeople who never achieved anything more than hearing their own false promises to themselves. These underachievers get all excited when their company announces some sort of sales incentive, boasting that they will surely win.

I worked at United States Properties with a salesman named Phil. Every month Phil enthusiastically announced that he was going to become salesman of the month, which would entitle him to some sort of monetary reward.

During the first week or so, Phil was motivated enough to work his butt off, uttering positive statements such as, "I'm really psyched to win this time," and "I know I am going to break all sales records for the month." By the time week three rolled around, Phil was unenthusias- tically mumbling excuses like, "Why break your ass for something that you will be too tired to enjoy," and "I can't catch the breaks like Arthur and Sam." (Arthur was myself; Sam was another successful salesman at United States Properties.)

What happens to salesmen like Phil? The answer is fairly simple. These salesmen are genuinely motivated and sincere when they com- mit themselves to a goal; what they lack is the persistence to continue their efforts when times get tough.

Set Your Own Course to Follow

Street smart sales pros develop the perseverance necessary to achieve greatness by clearly defining goals that they want to achieve, not goals that would please others. This is a critical point. Individuals who try to reach goals that others set will not be able to sustain their motivation. Oh, sure, they might at first appear to be enthusiastic and motivated in order to please the people who are important to them, but since they have not set these goals for themselves, these objectives become less and less important as they get harder and harder to reach.

Previously, we spoke about Phil, and how he wanted to become sales pro of the month. He was enthusiastic and motivated, especially after the company announced the incentive for that particular month. This was Phil's problem. He was only motivated after someone else set a goal for him. Phil never really had the deep-down desire to become a top sales producer. Inwardly, he knew that he did not have the perseverance to achieve that status; if he did, he would not need someone else to motivate him by setting sales goals for him. Street smart sales pros define their own personal goals, which have meaning to them.

I have a cousin, Richard, who dropped out of medical school in order to pursue an acting career. Needless to say, my aunt and uncle wanted to kill my cousin Richard. At the time, I myself doubted the wisdom of quitting—I was three years younger than Richard and struggling to pass all my college courses. A few years later, I had the opportunity to ask my cousin why he had made such a radical career move. Richard told me that he had always wanted to do something creative with his life. Whenever he had gone to a movie or theatre, he had envied the actors. The only reason he attempted to become a doctor was to please his parents, and the motivation to do so ran out shortly after that first year of medical school.

Looking back, I can clearly see that Richard made not only a brave decision, but a street smart one. We cannot live our lives for others, for that will surely lead us down a bitter road. Richard never made it as an actor, but by acknowledging his creative needs, he was eventually able to channel his talents into a highly successful career as an advertising executive. Be street smart—define where you want to go.

Just Do It

Street smart sales pros avoid procrastination; they do not put things off. Once they define what they want to achieve, they move quickly on their ideas. Good salespeople are aware that procrastination will inevitably lead to indifference. Individuals who are indifferent will never have the perseverance to reach their goals. When a person sets a goal, it is natural that his enthusiasm is strongest at the beginning of his efforts. This is the very reason that street smart sales pros react in a cobra-like fashion on their ideas.

The world is full of *could-have* millionaires who procrastinated their lives away. I had an uncle who swore to me that he thought of opening a fast food hamburger restaurant way before the McDonalds' chain was founded. Every time my uncle and I passed a McDonald's, he would invariably say, "Those restaurants *could have* been all mine. In fact, my hamburgers would have been ten times better than McDonald's." Whenever I questioned my uncle as to why he never pursued his idea to open a fast food restaurant, he would make one lame excuse after another and quickly change the subject to the second biggest disappointment in his life, the Dodgers moving out of Brooklyn.

Truth be told, my uncle never had the perseverance to allow himself the chance to achieve. He was a dreamer who became motivated for short periods of time. If someone had offered him a real opportunity, I'm sure he would have thought about it for so long that the opportunity would have disappeared. Street smart sales pros are doers, not procrastinators. Become a doer; be street smart!

Street smart sales pros do not need instant gratification in order to succeed. As a result of their enormous perseverance, street smart sales pros are fighters. They know how to roll with the punches. I am most proud that I never gave up during my first days of selling, even though I did not have a very encouraging beginning.

My very first sales appointment was with the Wilheim family. I was supposed to be at their home at seven in the evening in order to discuss some real estate opportunities that the company I worked for was offering. Not wanting to be late, I gave myself plenty of driving time in case I hit traffic. By five thirty, I was parked down the block from the Wilheim home. For the next hour and a half I practiced my sales presentation, trying to anticipate any objections that the Wilheims might come up with.

Finally, the witching hour arrived. Nervously, I adjusted my tie for the umpteenth time, pressed my tongue against my bottom front teeth (someone on a radio talk show once said that doing this helps to relieve tension, and in fact it does), took two deep breaths, and made my way to the Wilheims' front door.

I was greeted by Mr. Wilheim, a rather large man with a friendly enough smile. He brought me into his living room just as the evening news was coming on the television. As God is my witness, the following description of what happened to me in the next five minutes in the Wilheim home is one hundred percent true. I had just finished introducing myself to Mrs. Wilheim when a TV newsman began reporting on land frauds in the Pocono Mountains. Immediately, Mr. Wilheim's smile vanished. Even though I tried valiantly to inform him that my properties were not part of any land scams, and not remotely situated near the Pocono Mountains, he physically, and I mean physically, threw me out of his house. There I was on the sidewalk, sitting on my butt, humiliated and depressed!

The next day I awoke panic-stricken. My hands were covered with pimply, grotesque hives. Immediately I went to my doctor, fearing the worst. My doctor assured me that it was not serious—all I was suffering from was acute anxiety. Still, my hives were so bad that I had to wear white gloves to my next appointment. I looked like a Disney character.

All the same, I hit pay dirt. My next sales call was with a schoolteacher named George, who lived near Belmont race track in Queens, New York. I was instantly able to develop a rapport with George; being a former teacher, I am sure, was a great asset. Much to my delight, George was interested in my development and gave me a deposit on a piece of land. That following weekend, George came up to see the property. To my intense relief, he fell in love with it. George became my very first sale! My wife and I celebrated that evening, and amazingly enough my hives disappeared the following day, never to return again.

I have always attributed my success to the fact that my ability to persevere far exceeded my intellectual capacities. Underachievers look for instant gratification; they are incapable of persisting when things do not work out as they expected. If I had looked for instant gratification, I would have left the selling profession as soon as my butt hit the Wilheims' front walk. Be street smart—keep it up, become successful!

Consider This

In summary, street smart sales pros have the discipline to persevere in order to reach their goals. They develop this perseverance by setting goals that have meaning for them, not by trying to please others. They avoid procrastination by acting quickly on their ideas. Street smart sales pros are there for the long haul; they don't need instant gratification in order to sustain their motivation to succeed.

The following eight questions are designed to help you look within yourself to see if you are tough enough to become a street smart sales warrior. Persevere long enough to read these questions, think about them carefully, and answer them on a sheet of paper.

1. Specifically, what were the last few goals that you set for yourself which you failed to reach?

2. Why did you think you failed?

3. Do you find it more difficult to continue to take action in reaching a goal once your initial enthusiasm wears off?

4. If you had a choice, would you rather be doing something else with your life?

5. What, and why?

6. Is your performance hampered by procrastination?

7. If you do not succeed fairly quickly in reaching an objective, do you have a tendency to quit?

8. If so, why?

It is not always easy to look at the things that have not gone right in your life. It can be downright frightening. Bad memories, wrong decisions, unpleasant times—the thing to remember is that no one is immune to failure. Failure happens to everyone. If you don't think you can get past these emotional roadblocks, selling may not be for you. But if your answers are in line with what you've just read in this chapter, you've just taken a dramatic third step towards becoming a street smart sales pro!

4

Like What You See

Street smart sales pros have a lust for life, believing that each day brings new opportunities. Because of this attitude, they live each day as if it were their last, knowing that one day they will be right! These savvy sales pros never become so negative, depressed, or disgusted with themselves that they are not able to function at their highest level. If things do not go as expected on a given day, they write it off as a learning experience. Street smart sales pros understand that yesterday is a cancelled check, while today and tomorrow are opportunities to succeed—and street smart sales pros do indeed succeed!

The street smart sales pro has a strong self-image, which gives her enormous confidence in her ability to achieve. If your self-esteem is low and you find yourself walking around feeling depressed, frustrated, and so sorry for yourself that you can't function at a high level, then it is time for you to begin to develop a positive self-image. Be street smart—learn to *like what you see*!

Building Confidence

We already have suggested that a key element for the street smart sales pro to achieve great success is a positive self-image. But what factors actually influence the way a person sees herself? Why do some people have high self-esteem, while others have extremely low self-esteem? There are two important variables that influence the development of a person's self-esteem; one is internal and the other external. Let's look at both these factors a little more closely.

■ THE INTERNAL FACTORS

Most people become set in the way they see themselves by the time they are young adults. They have been greatly influenced by the way they have been raised. They could be victims of their childhoods, individuals who have rebelled against their parents' behaviors, or they could have had a perfectly normal upbringing—whatever that is. And as strange as it may seem, these childhood experiences do not necessarily determine how individuals see themselves when they are grown. All I know is that when I'm standing in front of a group of salespeople in a workshop, I can look into their faces and see who looks away and who has no difficulty responding to my questions. In these situations, the individual's self-esteem rises to the surface. I speak from experience: the way that people see themselves translates into either positive or negative behavior.

Underachievers do not see themselves as winners; they suffer from poor self-image. Their attitude about themselves is so negative that they sincerely believe that personal failure is unavoidable. They have so little faith in their abilities that they lack the confidence to try to overcome their problems. Underachievers believe their problems are insurmountable.

Underachievers reinforce their negative behavior by making statements such as, "I know I'm going to fail," "I'm not going to try that; there is no way I can accomplish that." These negative self-fulfilling prophecies rob the underachiever of any confidence or motivation he might have had.

For almost six months I worked with a saleswoman whom I will call Erica. She was the most self-effacing person I have ever met. It got to the point where I think she actually got some perverse pleasure out of putting herself down. Erica would even blame herself if it rained on a weekend, as if God had it in for her.

Sadly, I believe Erica had the potential to succeed, if only she had given herself a chance. Instead, she dwelled on the things that she did not like about herself, choosing not to see some of her positive attributes.

This is a crucial point. As a result of having a poor self-image, which combines negative thinking and a lack of confidence, many of us helplessly render ourselves into becoming salespeople like Erica. Underachievers do exactly that. They spend more time feeling bad about themselves, making all sorts of excuses why they can't achieve greatness, than time putting forth a total effort trying to overcome any of the problems they visualize.

Street smart sales pros see themselves as winners, and because of this they develop a positive self-image. They believe in their own abilities to succeed. If things do not go as expected, they don't punish themselves by putting themselves down. They never make destructive statements such as "I can't." Instead, they choose to say, "I can—and I will!"

Setbacks are viewed not as "that's the way my day is going," but rather as a challenge to the street smart sales pros. They do not feel sorry for themselves. Street smart sales pros understand that their problems are temporary roadblocks. They know that having a strong self-image, and continuing to think positively, will go a long way towards helping them to resolve any problems.

How many of you have become your own worst enemies by doubting your ability to achieve? Become street smart; wipe out ill feeling towards yourself. Speak in the positive: "I will succeed," "I know I can do that." Learn to like yourself!

Underachievers think that others around them see them as being inadequate, ineffective, and unqualified. This perspective is typical of individuals who have low self-esteem. After all, if they don't think much of themselves, why should they believe anyone else would?

Unfortunately, this negative view of how others see them only adds to the underachievers' depression, frustration, and despondency, making them feel nervous, uncomfortable, and embarrassed before they even have a chance to say hello to their new prospects! This defeatist attitude thoroughly destroys their confidence, making it difficult for the faker, taker, and maker to operate effectively on a day-to-day basis.

The street smart sales pro does not waste time worrying about how others see her; she is more concerned with keeping a positive self-image and getting the job done. She is bright enough to know that it's useless to have negative perceptions such as, "This client thinks I'm a jerk," or "Boy, am I embarrassing myself in front of this guy." There is nothing to be gained by this kind of thinking.

If things do not go well during a sales presentation, the street smart sales pro doesn't get embarrassed; she doesn't run and hide from that client. Instead, she learns from her experiences, salvaging whatever she can in order to try to get another opportunity to make the sale. She will not allow a poor presentation to squelch her motivation or confidence. She knows that sales pros do not go to jail just for giving lousy sales presentations—if they did, our jails would be bursting at the seams. It is important that you not waste your time worrying about what others think of you. Rather, concentrate on how you can improve your skills and develop a stronger, more confident self-image.

As part of many Japanese sales training programs, program directors insist that their sales pros sing a song in a crowded place, such as a train station. The purpose of this exercise is to build up a salesperson's self-confidence by proving to them that they are capable of surviving any potentially embarrassing experience. They get their salespeople to understand that there is really nothing to be ashamed about, and that negative feelings about themselves are merely flawed perceptions that they are perfectly capable of eliminating.

If you find yourself overly concerned with the way the world perceives you, it may be time for your singing debut. Stop worrying, and concentrate on getting the job done! You will find that people enjoy you more as soon as you are confident enough to give them a chance. Be street smart—learn to like yourself!

■ THE EXTERNAL FACTORS

External factors are influences created by the immediate social environment that surround us every day: attitudes of family, coworkers, employers, and other people we interact with on a regular basis. Just like internal factors, external factors can be translated into positive or negative behaviors, depending on the way the individual sees herself.

Street smart sales pros react positively to the external factors that influence them, whereas their underachieving counterparts react negatively to these same factors, giving themselves all sorts of excuses as to why they do not like their job, and why they are not able to perform.

One kind of external factor is the type of sales manager with whom an individual works, as this person can directly influence the way a sales pro performs. A poor sales manager allows mediocrity to become the standard for its sales department. A lax sales environment is comfortable to the underachiever. She doesn't feel threatened and is content to make the occasional small commission over and above her weekly salary. The lack of key supervision, combined with the security of having a check every Friday, hold the faker, taker, and maker in the job.

The street smart sales pro overcomes the negative influences of working with a poor sales manager by setting up her own standards of performance. These hard-working sales pros do not allow mediocrity to keep them from achieving great success. Picking up a paycheck every Friday, void of large commissions, offers no security to the street smart sales pro. The street smart sales pro is not on the job to take up space; she is not on the job because the environment is nonthreatening. She is on the job for one reason only: It provides her with the opportunity and satisfaction of earning big bucks, and if it didn't, she would move on to another job.

On the other hand, a strong sales manager can act as a positive external factor. A capable sales manager is conscientious, and realizes who is producing and who is not, knowing full well that it is her responsibility not to allow mediocrity to continue. Underachievers find it impossible to survive under a strong sales manager; due to their low self-esteem, they would interpret such a manager's most reasonable expectations as threatening, feeling that they are being picked on and shutting down when encouraged to produce more.

Street smart sales pros are only too happy to be working with capable sales managers. They see the manager as an integral part of their teams, working for the same positive results. Because the street smart sales pro has a strong self-image, she does not become defensive when her sales manager offers some constructive criticism or advice. Street smart sales pros are more concerned with the bottom line than with their ego. They are resourceful enough to take advantage of any help that is available.

I knew a salesman who sold all sorts of tools and gadgets to hardware stores. No matter how much or how little he sold, his income basically stayed the same. There were no performance incentives.

One year, he was offered a job by one of his competitors; through sales incentives, the job would have given him the opportunity to earn a great deal more money. Astonishingly, he turned the job down, for reasons that I now realize are typical of the underachiever. Instead of seeing opportunity, he chose to concentrate on what he perceived to be the negative aspects of the job. He was uncomfortable with the idea that he wouldn't have a guaranteed check waiting for him each week, even though he would be in a situation that could potentially pay him a lot more money.

He also voiced concern about the sales manager, who he felt could be very demanding. He liked being left alone; he did not want anyone on his back. Accountability was not for him. Seven years later, he is still on the job, living from paycheck to paycheck.

A street smart sales pro would have jumped at the opportunity to take a job that did not limit her earning potential. Street smart sales pros never think that they are going to fail—they believe in themselves, and that's all the security they need. Be street smart, be confident, be successful!

An external factor that directly influences fakers', takers', and makers' poor self-image is their feeling that they are always being looked at and put down by others. While this feeling is usually just in their minds, the fact is that the longer this attitude persists, the more likely that this paranoid behavior becomes noticeable. And as time goes by, people really do begin looking at them, because this paranoid behavior or negative performance tends to stand out.

Often, fakers, takers, and makers do not like their jobs because they have become bored with the product they are selling. Boredom totally wipes out any motivation that they might have had to sell, making it impossible for them to achieve success. Worse still, many salespeople simply do not believe in their product. This often occurs when sellers stop trying to learn enough about it. It is difficult to believe in something and remain excited if you have given up trying to discover all the positive things about it. Underachievers would rather complain and feel sorry for themselves, preferring to blame everyone in sight for their failures except the main culprit, themselves!

The street smart sales pro loves her job; if she didn't, she certainly would not choose to vegetate, feeling sorry for herself. Instead, she would go out and find a job she would enjoy.

Street smart sales pros love the challenge of becoming the very best in their companies. They find their work stimulating because it constantly creates new opportunities for them. Many times these enthusiastic sales reps will go after accounts that an underachiever would consider impossible to sell or a complete waste of time. Nevertheless, the street smart sales pros will try again and again and again to land one of these difficult accounts; and when they do, their enthusiasm and excitement for their work goes right through the roof!

It is important for the street smart sales pros to believe in the product they are selling. They are hustlers, not hucksters; they have to truly believe that their products can do the jobs they represent. These savvy sales pros never stop trying to learn more about their products. It helps to keep their enthusiasm and motivation high, giving them an edge over their competitors who have become bored, tired, and cynical.

About a year ago, on a Sunday afternoon, I was stretched out on my den couch eating pretzels, my favorite junk snack food, watching the New York Knicks attempting to beat the Boston Celtics. It was nearing the end of the fourth quarter in a close game when I heard my front doorbell ring. I quickly ran to answer it. Much to my dismay, standing on the front porch was a young man carrying a vacuum, with all sorts of attachments coming out from every angle of his body, giving him an alien-like appearance. This had to be a mistake. No one sells vacuums on a Sunday afternoon, especially during a Knicks-Celtics basketball game. Unfortunately for me, before I could get rid of this octopus of a sales pro, my wife, Sally, entered the hallway, greeted him, and quickly led this invader of my relaxation into the den to show us the vacuum.

For the next twenty minutes, this so-called salesman gave the most boring, unenthusiastic, monotonous sales presentation that I have ever had the dissatisfaction to witness. It was torture. If he had continued much longer I would have had to place toothpicks under my eyelids in order to keep my eyes from closing. I asked him straight out why he seemed to be so unhappy. This turned out to be my second biggest mistake of the day—the first being that I'd let him in.

He proceeded to whine to me, and I mean whine, about how he hated schlepping this vacuum around. It was obvious that the vacuum had become his enemy. When I asked him why he continued to do this kind of work if he hated it so much, he looked at me with a bewildered expression, replying that he really didn't know why, but probably because he needed a job and his cousin was the regional manager of the company. He was pathetic. Even if it had been the best vacuum in the world, there was no way that I would have bought it from him. Why encourage him to inflict his pain on other people?

If that vacuum sales pro had been street smart, he would have been enthusiastic and motivated to sell us. In addition, he would have treated that machine like priceless treasure, because in the hands of a street smart sales pro it would have been gold.

If you are disgusted with yourself and your job, and bored with the product you are selling, quickly look for a job that will make you feel good about yourself. Only then will you achieve; more importantly, you will begin to learn to like what you see in the mirror!

The negative thinking of others is the last external factor that can be extremely detrimental to the way a person sees her product, her company, and herself. As mentioned, people who are negative can dishearten and discourage individuals from trying to achieve. They tend to put people down with comments such as, "Don't try that," and "There is no way you can accomplish that."

If you have questions about any aspect of your job, never ask anyone who is negative for advice. These people are unhappy with themselves and are overjoyed upon hearing about others' problems. Their motto could easily be "misery loves company"—and believe me, they enjoy having loads of company.

Street smart sales pros talk only to people who can have a positive effect on them. They share their concerns with individuals who they believe genuinely care. Eleanor Roosevelt once said, "No one can make you feel inferior without your consent." The street smart sales pro fully understands this, and will not allow the negative thoughts of others to make her feel poorly about herself.

Consider This

Street smart sales pros have a positive attitude that enables them to achieve great success. These confident sales pros are more concerned with getting the job done than with worrying about what people think of them. They are problem solvers, not problem dwellers. They do not get so down on themselves that they are not able to achieve greatness. Street smart sales pros stay away from people who have a negative effect on their performance. Be street smart. If there is no one around for you to talk to who is positive, don't worry. Smile, look into the mirror, and discuss what's bothering you with someone you really like—yourself! Just remember not to do it with a lot of other people in the room.

The following ten questions are designed to see if you really like who you are. Be honest; the only one you can offend is yourself. So who cares? It's for your own benefit. Read these questions, think about them carefully, and answer them on a sheet of paper.

1. Do you have a positive or negative self-image?

2. How do you believe others perceive you?

3. Do you feel uncomfortable selling your product?

4. Do you believe you are living in the best of times?

5. If not, why not?

6. When you have a setback at work, do you become so depressed and despondent that you find it difficult to function at a high level in order to overcome any of those obstacles?

7. Are you more concerned with how you appear to others than you are with working towards getting the job done?

8. Do you tend to blame others for your misfortunes?

9. Are you being negatively influenced by the thoughts of others?

10. If so, how so?

Sometimes it is not easy to think about who you are. If you have low self-esteem or a pessimistic point of view, and find yourself surrounded by people who are negative, maybe you've hit upon the reason why you haven't achieved what you want. That in itself is a pretty good beginning. Now that you understand where these negative vibes are coming from, you have the ability to turn your negative self-image around. As soon as you understand the changes you have to make, you will be that much closer to becoming street smart!

5

Schtick

Street smart sales pros stand out. Why? Because of their schtick. But what is schtick? Schtick is a product of confidence—the ingenious methods by which the street smart sales pro distinguishes himself from the pack, marking himself as special. Schtick allows the street smart sales pro to be as creative as he wants, since schtick has no boundaries, restrictions, barriers, or limitations. Through the use of imagination and perseverance, the street smart sales pro is constantly trying to come up with a new schtick to set himself apart from his competition.

Since schtick can be interesting, exciting, or outrageous, work is always fun for the street smart sales pro. More important, shtick makes a sales pitch interesting and entertaining for the sales pro's prospects. This is a key point. The street smart sales pro entertains his customers, never offending them—and because they are entertained, the sales pro can get away with a lot of schtick!

If you are still using the same old selling techniques that you have used since you first started out (which by now have become boring and stale to you as well as to your prospects), it is time to develop schtick. Read this chapter with your imagination turned on, study some of the schtick that we will talk about, and get ready to have fun again in selling. Develop your own schtick; become street smart!

Street smart sales pros are the Walt Disneys of the sales profession, using their imaginations to come up with clever methods to gain an edge over their competition. Their clever techniques separate the skilled sales pros from the fakers, takers, and makers, who are as unique as white bread. Underachievers have to compete with everybody, since they never use their creativity to stand out from the crowd. The street smart sales pros' only competition is with themselves, and they are constantly trying to develop better ideas to create new sales.

When I first began selling recreational property, the company gave large monetary bonuses to any sales pros who sold a waterfront site. This interested me greatly; I wanted the big bucks. Instead of relying on company-generated leads, like everyone else, and hoping by chance that I would be lucky enough to get the one person who might buy that waterfront property, I decided to take things into my own hands, actively pursuing individuals who could afford such properties.

I made the decision to zero in on the medical community, knowing that this was one group that could easily afford these waterfront properties. I was aware that my most difficult task was to get doctors to take time out from their busy schedules to sit down long enough to listen to my presentation. I was confident that once I did get to see them, they would see the merits of having a place to escape to in order to relax—and what better place to relax than on the water?

After much thought, I decided to fill small Ziploc bags with a mixture of sand and coffee. I typed, dead center on blank white paper, a paraphrase of Will Rogers' famous line: "Land: once it's gone they can't manufacture it anymore," and simply signed my name underneath. A few days later I followed up my mailings with telephone calls, and was happy to discover that a large number of doctors came right to the phone without much effort on my part. They wanted to speak to the guy who went about sending dirt in the mail.

Initially, the other salesmen laughed at me when I went about filling my Ziploc packets with my earthen concoction. As I began selling waterfront after waterfront to all my newfound doctor friends, however, the laughter stopped. My schtick worked; it was not long before I became far and away the most successful salesman in the company. I soon learned that he who laughs last usually cashes the largest commission checks.

Imitate What Works

Street smart sales pros have the ability to learn from others. They make it a habit to study other imaginative and creative sales pros, figuring out how to use other techniques in order to improve upon their own performances. Not all street smart sales pros have the creative talents to develop an original effective schtick; some are clever enough simply to learn from others.

The great sales pros of history have always had great schtick. The one characteristic that great sales pros have in common is their willingness to come up with methods that clearly set them apart from their competition. Most of the time, finding the right schtick is a trial-and-error process. This is a key point: it is very rare that an achiever will come up with a schtick that will prove to be a winner on the first attempt. Sometimes a little fine tuning is necessary—and other times, major revisions.

Through their imagination, motivation, and perseverance, street smart sales pros all have developed unique selling techniques that have made them champions in each of their fields. These creative selling techniques may not be right for your personality; however, the purpose of studying other people's imaginative ideas is to stimulate your own creative juices.

■ A VALUABLE FIVE MINUTES

Ben Feldman has sold nearly a billion dollars' worth of life insurance. Feldman found that his most difficult task was to get a chief executive officer (CEO) of a major corporation to sit down and listen to his presentation.

The technique Ben came up with was quite clever. Whenever he arrived at an office without having an appointment, he would hand the CEO's secretary an envelope containing five $100 bills and would ask for five minutes of the man's time. In one particular case that Feldman cites, he got in to see the executive and eventually sold him $50 million worth of life insurance. Asked about his greatest sale, Feldman replied, "I don't know. I haven't made it yet." This is a street smart attitude at its very best.

■ THE CARD

For fourteen years, Joe Girard sold an average of eighteen cars a week—this does not include fleet sales—making him the most successful car sales pro ever. Joe was always prospecting and selling, no matter where he was. Whenever Joe attended a sporting event, he would bring thousands and thousands of business cards, which he would toss in the air whenever the crowd stood to applaud a special play. Invariably, someone at the game either needed or knew someone who wanted to buy a new car. Joe took advantage of every possible opportunity.

■ THE ROSE

I worked with a sales pro named Lenny Bieler. Lenny's schtick was to give his prospects one red rose. Often, their first response was anything but positive, questioning why Lenny would bother them with this sort of nonsense. Calmly, Lenny would reply, "I have been trying to see you for the longest of times, and because you are so busy I needed my friend the rose to help me out, and I guess it worked. Now that I am here, believe me, I am glad I did bring my friend along." Lenny would then go into his presentation, and the majority of times his prospects appreciated this clever approach, giving Lenny the opportunity needed to achieve success.

■ THE RIBBON

The key to the success of a college book sales representative is to get his text books read by the department's course coordinators, who make the decisions on which books will be used the following year. College professors do not want to sit through sales presentations, preferring to have the various book salesmen leave their texts behind so that they can peruse them at their own convenience. Since there are so many other salespeople leaving their books, it is virtually impossible for a professor to evaluate each and every book. Accordingly, the problem Jenna Famiglietti had to overcome was to get that department head to read *her* book.

The schtick used by our clever book sales pro was rather simple. Like everyone else, Jenna would leave her textbooks on the professor's desk, but with a critical difference: she would tie a bright green ribbon around each of her books. Guess whose books were always read? This schtick made our book saleswoman tops in her field.

■ THE LOOK

The key to selling consulting services is to get to see the chief executive officer, who for the most part is extremely busy. He has no interest in hearing how other people are going to show him how to run his company more efficiently. To get to see these executives is next to impossible, unless you're Bob McAfee.

The schtick used by Bob was to let his apparel do the talking for him. He would walk into the outer office of the CEO that he wanted to see, never having an appointment, and announce to the executive secretary that he would like to see the person who ran the company. His schtick was his outfit: he would always be dressed formally in a three-piece suit, wearing a brown derby hat, all the while carrying a black lacquered walking cane with highly polished gold tips.

Instead of brushing him off, these executive secretaries would run off to ask their bosses if they would like to talk to a rather odd-looking gentleman. You might be self-conscious dressing in this manner, but I can tell you this: that brown derby and walking stick got Bob to see an awful lot of top CEOs, helping our consulting sales pro earn large commission checks.

■ THE GREED IS GOOD CIGAR

In the classic 1987 movie *Wall Street*, Charlie Sheen portrays Bud Fox, a young up-and-coming stockbroker. Bud has been desperately trying to set up an appointment with Gordon Gekko, a powerful financier, played by Michael Douglas. Realizing that his efforts would be fruitless if he continued to try and see Douglas through conventional means, he decided to use some schtick to make it happen.

After doing some research, Bud was able to find out when Gekko's birthday was. He waited for his opportunity, and the day of his birthday Bud showed up at Gekko's office carrying a box of very expensive cigars, informing Mr. Gekko's secretary that he would like to hand-deliver his present. The secretary took the box of cigars and walked into the financier's office, quickly returning with the news Bud wanted to hear: Gekko had said that Bud just bought himself five minutes. Bud's schtick worked; five minutes was all the time he needed!

I knew a sales pro who used the library as a source in order to develop an effective schtick. He had zero personality, and he knew it, which in a way made him very street smart. This fellow took out a book of jokes, which he in turn memorized. His schtick soon became that of a comedian. His customers looked forward to seeing him, knowing that he would have one or two jokes to tell them.

The key point is that schtick can come from anywhere. It can be corny, funny, thought-provoking, entertaining, attention-grabbing, and clever. Use it and set yourself apart from your competition. These sales pros are excellent examples of how using creativity helps salespeople stand out from the crowd. You can get ideas for shtick by watching other sales pros, or you can develop schtick by reading books or magazines, or even by watching a movie. Do what it takes to find a shtick that works!

Consider This

Street smart sales pros are aware that no one ever became a leader in his field by doing what was expected. Rousseau once said, "The world of reality has its limits; the world of imagination is boundless." Use your imagination; become street smart!

The following eight questions are designed to help you start to use your creativity. Don't be afraid to use your imagination. This doesn't mean that you have to become a raving lunatic or do something offensive to be noticed. Tying a green ribbon around a text book was not outrageous, but nevertheless, proved to be a very effective tool for our saleswoman. The schtick that you employ should be in keeping with your own personality. The important thing is for you to be creative and not continue to be an ordinary Joe or Jill. Be original—it will earn you those large commission checks.

Read these questions, think about them carefully, and answer them on a sheet of paper.

1. Do you have any schtick?

2. Do you know anyone else who has schtick?

3. If so, what?

4. Would you find it uncomfortable as well as embarrassing to use a sales method that was out of the ordinary?

5. If so, why?

6. Can you think of anything to do that can set you apart from your competition?

7. If not, why not?

8. Where would you look to find some inspiration for developing your own creative selling techniques?

Now that you have finished reading this chapter, you know how important it is to develop a selling technique that will set you apart from your competition. If you find that creative selling would not be too uncomfortable or embarrassing, but rather a lot of fun, you have taken a major step towards becoming street smart.

6

Money-Making Rejection

Street smart sales pros have an enormous amount of resilience, which enables them to deal with rejection on a daily basis. Day after day, their potential customers knowingly or unknowingly beat them down in some fashion, but these street smart sales pros persist long enough to walk away with large commissions.

Fakers, takers, and makers can't deal with rejection very well; it sends them right to their psychiatrists' couches. Underachievers need to have the approval of others. They base their self-worth upon it. Street smart sales pros know that basing your self-worth upon others' approval is nonsense. Their goal is self-approval, trusting their own actions.

These self-confident sales pros are aware that having an attitude like the underachiever's will only beget a life of misery and frustration, making it impossible for them to handle rejection, because in a sense they will be rejecting themselves. Street smart sales pros know that if you are going to succeed and stay in sales for the long term, it is essential for you to deal positively with rejection. The greater your ability to handle failure and rejection on a daily basis, the more likely you are to achieve greatness.

The Power of "No"

If you are finding it difficult to motivate yourself after hearing the word "no" from one of your prospects, it is time to learn how to deal positively with rejection. Street smart sales pros never take rejection personally. When a prospect says "no" to a street smart sales pro, she interprets it as a challenge to try to overcome her prospect's objections in order to make the sale.

When a client says "no," the street smart sales pro understands this to mean, "maybe," "perhaps," or, "Tell me more, I'm not convinced yet." Street smart sales pros never, never, never consider "no" to mean, "I definitely will never do business with you." This is the very reason why they have no difficulty going back time and again to their prospects.

When will a street smart sales pro finally give up? When her customers decide to enunciate the word "yes"!

Fakers, takers, and makers are totally destroyed when they get rejected. These underachievers hear the word "no" so loudly it reverberates in their heads as in an echo chamber. Underachievers take rejection so personally at times that they are hesitant to even ask for an order because of their fear of hearing the word "no." When they hear the word "no," they interpret it as, "This guy hates me," "He thinks I'm stupid," or "He'll never want to see me again."

My father has a cousin who used to sell piece goods, that is, textile products. According to my dad, his cousin's greatest asset as a salesman was the fact that he never took "no" for an answer. He would keep going back to the very same accounts that continually rejected him, until finally he wore them down and was able to get an order. Like my dad's cousin, the street smart sales pro believes just because someone says "no" one time, it doesn't mean he will say "no" the next time.

Astonishingly, most children, before entering school, start off as street smart sales pros. They never hear the word "no." Kids are not looking for the approval of others; "no" doesn't phase them in the least. They come back again and again, nagging a parent to death in order to get their way. And like the street smart sales pros who are able to persevere, on many occasions kids are able to wear down their parents in order to close their sales!

What turns a child who handles rejection easily into a nervous wreck who crumbles the minute she suspects the least bit of rejection? It begins when we enter grade school, leaving behind the security of mommy and daddy, who love us to death and think everything we do is cute. We start playing with other children, and quickly learn that the kids who may be a little different, not quite adjusted to leaving mommy, are the ones who get picked on and go home to cry each day. We don't want this grief; we want to be liked; and we'll do almost anything to be accepted. Underachievers, like the grade school child, will do almost anything to gain the approval of others. Fakers, takers, and makers have never been able to overcome their fear of rejection.

The street smart sales pro also wants to be accepted by her peers, but as she gets older she puts limits on this desire. She will not allow peer pressure to negatively influence her performance. Even as a young adult, the street smart sales pro knew that the need to be liked was not as important as liking herself!

Learn from Rejection

Street smart sales pros are not afraid to find out why they did not get the order. They have learned that many prospects are more than willing to tell them why they don't want to do business with them. Street smart sales pros realize that this information can be invaluable and can potentially be used at that very moment to overcome a client's objection in order to make a sale. And even if the street smart sales pros cannot use the information immediately to make a sale, they certainly can use it in the future. The key is finding out what the problem is and working on fixing it—be it delivery, quality, price, or their performance as sales pros.

Street smart sales pros are not so sensitive to rejection that they will allow criticism to damage their chances of making money with that particular client in the future. Underachievers, upon hearing the word "no," quickly pack up their wares and leave their prospect, too afraid to find out exactly why they did not get the order. Because of their fear of rejection, they lose many future opportunities for themselves.

A clever technique that the street smart sales pro employs in order to avoid the frustrations that are associated with rejection, is to put a money value on every presentation that she makes. Therefore, the street smart sales pro believes she earns money even if she does not close a sale. This well-adjusted sales pro knows that no one is able to sell everybody the first time, and expects to get a certain amount of "no" responses before she gets a "yes."

Money-Making Rejection

Let's suppose a sales pro earns a thousand dollars in commission every time she completes a sale. In this particular example, this sales pro is aware that she sells one out of four prospects that she sees. If that be the case, how much money did she earn if she saw three people who did not buy from her? Underachievers will always say that the sales pro did not earn anything. The street smart sales pro, on the other hand, will always say that she earned $750; each "failed" prospect took her one step nearer to the thousand dollar payload. That is why she never feels rejected on a sales call. She knows that every "no" that she gets on a sales call gets her that much closer to a "yes."

In the example above, the street smart sales pro understands that over the year her closing percentage would be one out of four. Before she makes a sale, she will get three "no" answers. That is why she is convinced that every sales presentation that she makes is earning her money. It is part of the job. It's part of the process that she has to go through before she reaches her goal, so why not get paid for it? She chooses to call a presentation that is not successful a *money-making rejection.*

Consider This

If every prospect said "yes" the first time a salesperson were to solicit her, there would be a hell of a lot more people out there selling things. The fact that many prospects do say "no" provides the street smart sales pro with a golden opportunity that the underachievers don't see. Street smart sales pros know that rejection is part of life, and the greater their abilities to handle rejection, the more likely they will be to achieve success.

Be street smart—never reject yourself in order to gain the approval of others. Do not take it personally when you hear the word "no" from one of your prospects. Remember, to the street smart sales pros, a "no" today is a "yes" tomorrow!

The following questions are designed to give you some insight as to the effect that rejection may have on your performance. Read these questions, consider them carefully, and answer them on a sheet of paper.

1. Do you find that it is important for you to be accepted by others, even though it may require you to reject some of your own ideas?

2. If so, why?

3. Do you get depressed when a client says "no" to you?

4. How many times would you go back to a client before giving up?

5. Would you feel uncomfortable asking a client why he would not do business with you?

6. If so, why?

Now that you have finished reading this chapter, you know that the word "no" in sales has many different connotations to the street smart sales pro, who knows never to take this rejection personally.

If you still find that it is too depressing to handle the day-to-day rejection that is part and parcel of sales, you are not alone. I will tell you a secret: As excited as I may have been to make my first few sales, I understood how frustrating a "no" could be, especially having been physically ejected from a prospect's home. I just figured that all I needed was a chance to get up to bat; even if I struck out, I knew I would eventually get a hit. You might think differently, in which case sales may not be for you. However, if you have found that your answers are in line with the thinking in this chapter, then you have taken a sixth giant step towards becoming a street smart sales pro!

PART II

Tools of the Street Smart Sales Pro

Before you turn your attention away from Part One, I want you to understand that each and every one of the elements that I wrote about in the previous part is important if you are going to achieve greatness. However, only when these elements are integrated into your method of selling will they prove invaluable to you.

The process of putting together the elements of selling is a lot like learning to drive. The first time you sat behind the wheel of a car, each element of driving felt like a completely different act: stepping on the gas to accelerate; braking to slow down; looking into your rear view mirror, then side mirror; and, of course, steering the car in the right direction. At first, each of these actions seemed to require its own separate skill set. But with enough practice, they all eventually began to meld together, making driving seem like a single, unified, natural act. The same holds true for the elements necessary for selling. You might have to practice each element separately until you find that you are comfortable with each one. Once that happens, the elements will all soon become integrated into the person who you are and who you want to become.

So now that you know the necessary elements that make a street smart sales pro a true champion, how do you go about building up your own client list? To build most anything, you need the right tools. In the second half of the book, I will provide you with all the tools you will ever need. These tools are the tactics employed by street smart sales pros to make it happen—to get from point A (having a product or service) to point B (making the sale) by finding and capitalizing on a good prospect.

I love this part because it provides salespeople with the ability to be creative, to find their own niche, and to excel at selling. Because each one of us is different and the products or services we sell vary greatly, I understand that not every tool can work for everybody. Therefore, I have made sure to include a wide selection of tried-and-true tactics from which to choose. As you put these tactics to work, if you find that one doesn't work for you, try the next; and if that one doesn't work, move on to the one that does. The idea is to find the right tactics that fit into your personality, product, or service.

Carried out correctly, these tactics will not only transform the way you sell, but they will also make you a street smart sales pro and provide you with all the lovely perks that go along with that status.

7

Prospecting

To a street smart sales pro, prospecting is like looking for gold. Instead of digging into the earth, however, prospecting is searching for individuals who have the need and the ability to purchase a product or service. Like the prospector who stakes his claim, a sales pro with a rich supply of qualified leads has the potential to earn his fortune.

A sales pro without leads or people to talk to is like a fish without water. Neither can survive very long. Yet a common problem among most salespeople is a lack of sufficient leads. Underachievers have a great deal of difficulty deciding where to find qualified prospects. Well, where do all those wonderful leads come from? Good question—no—excellent question. Let me tell you. Those wonderful leads normally stem from four methods.

First, though this is rare in today's market, your product may be in such demand that it practically sells itself. More often, this occurs when a particular type of product—smartphones, electronic tablets, energy drinks, or natural supplements, for example—becomes a national must-have item.

Second, the company you are working for may have its own in-house marketing program that will produce leads through its promotion on websites, media, direct mail, or print advertising. A company such as Avon is a good example of a company that spends a lot of dollars to generate a good supply of qualified leads for its salespeople.

The third way leads can come is from your own personal circle of friends, family, and acquaintances. Some industries base their sales projections on the principle that new sales reps will initially sell to many people that they know. These companies are constantly hiring because of this fact. They also know that many salespeople will fail once they burn through the people they know.

The fourth is to acquire leads from companies that specialize in selling listings to salespeople. Look up "business leads" in your search engine, and you will find the websites of companies that have access to tens of thousands of businesspeople and professionals. These lists can include specified business categories, company names, individual names, positions, addresses, emails, phone numbers, and more. Some companies can also break down lists by sex, income level, geographical location, and general interests. Not only can you find lists covering North America, certain companies can provide lists covering the rest of the world. Always make sure that you work with a reputable company and that you compare prices. Please keep in mind that the contacts generated are considered blind leads, which means that they have not been qualified as needing a product or service such as yours.

In contrast to the conventional four methods of getting leads, there is a fifth way, one that separates the achievers from the underachievers. Street smart sales pros learn never to count on the first four sources of leads. They know that they themselves are the greatest sources of their own leads.

Part of the problem facing underachievers is that they do not know how to prospect on their own. They have counted so heavily in the past on company support for their leads that they have failed miserably in developing their own program. When for whatever reason their company has a short supply of leads, the sales production of these underachievers goes down dramatically. Street smart sales pros will not allow this to happen. They do not depend solely on in-house leads or an outside company's computer-generated leads. When other salespeople are sitting around the office hoping to see clients, street smart sales pros are busy telling their stories to qualified buyers. These adroit sales pros know that using their own methods of outreach can benefit them and their companies in both the short and long run.

Getting Leads the Street Smart Way

If you are currently dependent on others to produce leads for you, read this chapter carefully. Discover all the outside sources that are available so that you can develop your own lead-generation program. Learn the street smart tactics for prospecting. No longer will you wake up on a particular day and not know where to go or with whom to talk. Be street smart, pan for the gold; it will be well worth your effort.

■ REFERRALS

Street smart sales pros are keenly aware that a prospect referred by an existing client who is happy with your product or service is a heck of a lot easier to sell than a new lead who knows very little about you and your company. Understanding this, street smart sales pros use their existing client base to obtain many qualified leads.

There is a skill in asking customers for referrals. Merely requesting, "Do you know anyone who can use my service?" rarely does the trick. This is because you are asking that client to make a judgment as to whether he knows someone who is ready to buy your product or service. In most instances, it is not possible for him to know. That is the reason why many clients, even those with the best intentions, will instinctively answer "no." It's similar to a knee-jerk response.

Aware of this, street smart sales pros ask clients if they belong to any business organizations, clubs, charities, etc. This is done for several reasons: to see if the client is fully engaged outside of his own office, to see if there are any common connections upon which to build a relationship, and to learn if there are other groups our pro is not aware of that in which he might consider participating.

If the street smart sales pro's client is in an office building that has other tenants, he asks if the client has any other business connections located in the building that he could drop by to see. The theory behind this is simply that most of us surround ourselves with individuals who have similar interests, earning power, preferences, and needs. By asking for referrals in this manner, your client doesn't have to think of anything more than supplying you with names. And that's the name of the game—getting people to talk to. Remember, it is your job to do the qualifying and selling, not your client's job.

Street smart sales pros know that the best time to ask for referrals is right after the sale. At that point, your customer's enthusiasm and satisfaction are at their highest. When I feel that I have developed a strong rapport with a client, I often ask him if he would mind telephoning his friends and telling them about me. If a client responds that he is not comfortable doing this or he's too busy, I then ask him if it is okay if I use his name when telephoning. In some cases, he might indicate that he also would not be comfortable with this, in which case I wouldn't use his name. In most cases, however, you will find that your customers will only be too happy to help you.

Because referrals are so essential to your success, you should always stay in touch with your old clients. Send them birthday and holiday cards. Record such dates in your electronic calendar. Call or email them to see how they are doing. If the client is having a problem, take care of it promptly. Stop in to see them. Let them know that you haven't forgotten them simply because they already bought. Never take a client's business for granted, and make sure to reach out regularly for referrals.

Be street smart; never forget that every person who owns or uses your product or service just might know someone who could utilize it as well.

■ BIRD-DOGS

A bird-dog is a dog that finds birds for hunters before and after they are shot from the sky. A sales bird-dog is an individual who beats the bushes, so to speak, in order to find qualified prospects for a sales pro, who will pay him a commission or otherwise reward him if he helps to make the sale. Bird-dogs can be extremely effective. They will speak to everybody just so they get an opportunity to make some extra money.

Bird-dogs can be relatives, friends, secretaries, past clients, postal workers, etc. These individuals can be much more effective than any computer when it comes to finding leads. You will see quickly that it pays to enlist as many bird-dogs as you can. It's the street smart thing to do.

▮ NETWORKING

Networking is the art of reaching out to others who may have common interests and forming business relationships for mutual benefit. The most successful sales pros have always used this tactic to their maximum advantage, and opportunities for networking have only gotten better over the years. There are three levels of networking. The first and oldest is quite basic, but is relatively effective if used correctly. The second involves work, but expands the sales pro's reach to a much wider community-based audience. The third level utilizes the computer to access a whole universe of people interested in creating new opportunities. Let's examine each level.

Friendly Conversation

Through the course of a week, you may run into twenty or thirty people whom you know or whom you may meet for the first time. This includes your barber, attorney, banker, plumber, landlord, and friends. When you do, engage them in conversation and ask them about their job and how things are going, then tell them what you do for a living. Ask if there is anyone they know who can use your product or service. Of course, I will admit that if you network repeatedly with the same people in a heavy-handed way, these people might wish to avoid you. On the other hand, if you do it correctly and show interest in what they do, they will reciprocate. Some may in fact, bird-dog for you. This approach may be low-tech, but it works.

Becoming a Joiner

Throughout North America there are many activity-based or social organizations that bring together individuals with the purpose of either doing community service or networking—and often both. These organizations include charities, civic groups, professional societies, religious congregations, volunteer work, etc. Sometimes business networking is integrated with community projects, as with service organizations like the Rotary, Lions, and Kiwanis clubs. There are also national, regional, and local business networks that are specifically designed to assemble businesspeople to interact and develop new contacts at meetings, workshops, and lectures; the Business Networking Institute (BNI) is a good example of such a group.

By joining several organizations, sales pros maximize their networking abilities, putting themselves in contact with many potential clients. And by becoming active members and raising their visibility in a group, sales pros greatly increase their exposure. For more examples of some well-known social and business groups, please consult the Resource section on page 193.

Two additional areas in which street smart sales pros should consider participating are golf outings and country clubs. It is no secret that a good deal of business gets done on the golf course. By visiting a course and meeting others who play golf, the sales pro can develop a continuing source of new leads. And while becoming a member of a country club can be expensive, it can pay off handsomely. Country clubs offer a unique opportunity to meet people who are movers and shakers within their own businesses.

And last but not least are gyms, weight-loss centers, professional workshops, and adult education programs. These are perfect places to meet new people while at the same time improving both one's body and mind.

E-Networking

The Internet has opened up many unique ways for the street smart sales pro to reach out, giving him the potential to find thousands of new prospects with the click of a button. The process of connecting online is called e-networking, and can render fantastic results when used properly. By expanding your circle of contacts—from friends and family to new clients and business partners—you allow yourself unprecedented access to new markets.

Don't discredit the power of social media platforms like Facebook and Twitter. These sites are not just spaces for you to post pictures of your kids and pets—they allow you to maintain your existing relationships with friends, family, and clients, and also give you the opportunity to meet new prospects through your existing contacts. By setting up a profile for yourself or your company, you create an easy way for prospects new and old to contact you and keep up with your company's products and services. Although blatant selling does not usually work, subtle mentions can be quite effective in spreading the word about a product or individual. In addition, these social media platforms can keep you up to date on the latest trends and preferences. Social networks also afford you the chance to humanize yourself; they let your personal style or sense of humor shine through in an informal setting, making clients feel more of an emotional connection to you and your product or service. The more a prospect likes or admires you as a person, the more likely he is to buy from you.

There are also specific networking sites devoted to developing business networks for like-minded individuals. By far the leading professional networking site is LinkedIn.com. With a membership of over two hundred million, LinkedIn provides sales pros with the ability to find and interact with businesspeople and professionals. LinkedIn allows sales pros to locate business leads according to interest, to communicate with hard-to-find individuals, and to advertise their experience and expertise.

You could join any of a number of casual online communities devoted to sports, hobbies, volunteer work, etc. For every interest that exists, there's a webgroup devoted to discussing it, be it a fansite on the Yankees or a privately run forum whose mission is to save Abdulali wrinkled frogs in India. What are your interests? Cultivate them online, and not only will you make new friends, but you'll also discover hundreds of potential new clients

And as a final option—if you don't mind doing a little web surfing—there are many free listings of potential customers available on the Internet everywhere. Many businesses, manufacturers, and groups display comprehensive listings of the customers and clients to promote the fact that they have worked with, serviced, or distributed to these operations. In some cases, they provide listings of their membership. A number of online telephone directories will group together specific professionals, companies, or retailers based on your search request.

Sales pros know that these lists can be gathered by putting the name of any group into a search engine and looking through the results. Once the names of potential clients are found, the Internet can also provide background information about the company or individual—information that can be extremely valuable when initiating contact. While others may have done the footwork in gathering these lists, sales pros can reap the benefits by doing their due diligence before following up.

■ DEVELOPING YOUR WEB PRESENCE

Joining a social or business network is just one way that the street smart sales pros maximize their business exposure online. This exposure is called web presence, and can be increased in many other ways.The Internet provides sales pros with the ability to be seen and heard on a continuing basis, twenty-four hours a day, seven days a week.

In the digital age, a website is the most important Internet tool a sales pro can have. By setting up a website or blog from which to communicate thoughts, ideas, and promotions to others, the street smart sales pro makes sure he is never out of sight. The appearance of your website is important—for many, it is the only indication of the quality of the product or service they hope to receive. Prospects judge on appearances; if your website is clunky, slow, ineffective, and aesthetically undistinguished, your customer will assume your product is, too. The more refined and accessible your website is, the more likely you are to gain a new customer. Spend the money for a professional web designer who will create an attractive, informative website for yourself or your company; as your virtual "face," this site will go a long way towards establishing your online credibility. If you cannot afford to hire a private web designer, there are a number of web service providers that provide all the assistance necessary to set up a solid, good-looking site with all the requisite bells and whistles.

In addition, there are consumer-based websites and services devoted to evaluating and promoting businesses. Traditionally, agencies such as the Better Business Bureau have served as mediators between customers and businesses, allowing people to find good, reliable companies that will provide the services that they need. You can ask that you or your company be listed on their website and evaluated accordingly; a plaudit from the Better Business Bureau is usually considered a mark of distinction, and can help new prospects locate and do business with you. Increasingly, other crowd-sourced online directory services such as Yelp or Angie's List also allow customers to find and review local businesses. After you make a sale, ask your client to write you a good review on Yelp or Angie's List, if she is a member. These positive reviews can go a long way toward helping new customers choose you and your product and service.

The street smart sales pro has a substantial web presence, including a website, Twitter feed, Facebook page, and listings on multiple business evaluation sites. This farsighted sales pro knows that in order to make inroads on the Internet business world, it is essential to maintain a high profile online. Be street smart—expand your web presence. Miss the opportunities that the Internet provides, and you'll be missing a very big chance to make money.

■ TRADING LEADS

An excellent method of prospecting is to set up a system that allows you to trade leads with other sales pros who sell to the same market as you. For example, home improvement and appliance sales pros can have an effective trading program, because people who have work done on their homes are often in the market for new appliances, and the reverse is also true.

Analyze who your customers are, and then create a list of all the complementary products or services they might utilize. After your list is compiled, you can go about trying to set up a trading network between you and the other sales pros. Internet sites can put you into contact with others who are willing to trade lists; however, always make sure you know who you are dealing with on the other end. Be choosy about the people you do business with; you want to get quality leads from your trading partner, and you certainly don't want to see your own list posted online the next day.

■ PROSPECTING BY EMAIL

Today, more and more people prefer to conduct their business online, learning about and purchasing new products or services over the Internet. As you develop your web presence, you'll find that you start to get more client inquiries about your product or service by email, not by phone call. Linked as part of your website's contact information, email thus becomes an essential way to develop and keep in touch with your client base.

Email offers many advantages over telephone or door-to-door prospecting. The primary advantage is that it increases your availability to your customers. Office hours may be limited, or a customer may operate in a distant time zone; email gives both sales pros and their clients the opportunity to communicate at any hour of the day. Email also offers speed and efficiency, allowing you to cut to the chase with a brief, succinct inquiry or response. The street smart sales pro knows he can use those extra hours to develop more client relationships! In addition, email can help you cut costs—a long-distance call to Brazil isn't cheap, but an email to Brazil is free! Finally, email allows you to reach more people than ever before—with a single email or e-newsletter, you can keep hundreds of people up-to-date on your most current deals and offerings.

Email need not be spam. The street smart sales pro knows how to write an email that will not be deleted on sight. By personalizing his messages, and by keeping them short and informative, the street smart sales pro uses email to make the most of the virtual business world. Be street smart—use email effectively!

Business Email Etiquette

We've all been there. You wake up in the morning and go to check your email, only to find your inbox flooded with junk messages— "Buy Our Supplement Now!," "Work From Home—Make $5,000 a Week!," or "Donate to Senator Jingleheimer's Campaign!" People use email to search for new prospects every day: We call these emails spam. In fact, spamming has become so common that most people delete, block, or ignore these electronic expressions of desperation. As the number of spam emails has increased, the interest on the part of recipients has decreased.

The street smart sales pro knows that spamming is no way to drum up business. Yet there is considerable value to using email; in the right hands, email can be a very powerful tool for finding and interacting with new prospects. How do you write a business email that will get noticed?

The key to successful business emailing is to keep things personal. Unless you're sending an e-newsletter, do not send out group emails; write to one person at a time. People like to think they're special—nothing gets deleted faster than an email that's obviously a form message sent to dozens of other prospects. You may set up a template for initial business inquiries, but tailor it to the specific identity of your prospect. How do you know this person? Were you referred by a friend, family member, coworker, or client? Did you meet her through a networking group, community service organization, or golf club outing? Use this connection to reaffirm your relationship to the prospect and keep her engaged. Also, reference the connection in your subject line—your prospect is less likely to ignore an email that comes from a friend of her uncle Bob.

In personalizing your email, be casual—but not too casual. Business emails need not be stiff and boring; however, a certain level of formality should be maintained. Your email should be properly spelled and punctuated, and have both a greeting and a closing. Feel free to add a little humor to your message, but avoid inappropriate jokes, political overtones, or overly forward remarks. Don't write with lowercase letters only, and for goodness' sake, don't use emoticons. A business email should not resemble a note to your third-grade pen pal.

Keep the email short. Nobody has the patience to wade through a long narrative; your email should be three or four paragraphs at most. A business inquiry is not the time to recap the narrative of last night's HBO special. Greet your prospect, reaffirm your relationship, explain briefly why you think your product or service would serve her well, and finish up.

And remember that the purpose of your email is almost always to set up a face-to-face appointment or meeting with your prospect. While some sales can be discussed and closed entirely over email, nine times out of ten, you'll want to be able to see the prospect in person or talk to her on the phone in order to make a stronger appeal. Accordingly, make sure to provide different ways for the prospect to respond to your email; she'll have your email address, obviously, but give her your cell phone and office numbers, too, in case she prefers to talk on the phone.

The idea is to use the email as a platform for setting up a more extensive discussion of your product or service in the future.

Additionally, you may want to use your email to indicate that you are available not only for the prospect, but for anybody the prospect knows who might also be interested in your product or services. An email can plumb deep new business connections, if used correctly.

When a prospect emails you back, reply within twenty-four hours, even if it's just to say that you are backlogged and will respond more extensively at a slightly later time. Business moves quickly in the digital world; we're all so plugged in that clients have come to expect prompt attention. A tardy response makes you come across as lazy or disinterested—not the kind of person who gets the sale!

Finally, follow up! If *you* don't hear back from your prospect, send another email to see why no response was received. Busy people have full inboxes; despite your best efforts, sometimes your message will get lost in the shuffle. Don't be afraid to send a second message reminding your prospect about your company. Establishing a line of communication is critical.

Here's a sample email:

Subject: It's Tim from the Kiwanis Club

Dear Ellis,

It was great seeing you and your wife the other night at the charity auction. I'm so glad we got a chance to talk—and hear Frank sing "You Are So Beautiful," of course!

You mentioned that you wished that you could do something about speeding up production at your company. As it turns out, my company, Binky Widgets, has just released the Binky 3000, which does five widgety things better, faster, and more reliably than the other widgets on the market. I think you'll appreciate how the new Binky can help improve your production efficiency.

I'll give you a buzz on Wednesday to set up a meeting. In the meantime, if you have any questions, you know how to reach me. Now if only we could teach Frank how to sing on key!

Best,
Todd Vucevic

E-newsletters

Believe it or not, there is one kind of mass email that can actually serve you well—the e-newsletter. The e-newsletter can be very effective as a tool for keeping your client base informed about all the latest products, promotions, and happenings. The street smart sales pro knows that the better informed his clients are, the more likely they are to buy again.

Build your email list around clients who you know will want to hear more from you or your company. When you meet a prospect, ask him if he wants to join the list in order to learn more about your business; when you close a sale, ask the client if he'd like to be kept up-to-date on new deals as they come up. Include friends, family members, and bird-dogs who might suggest other potential e-newsletter recipients. Your email list will only grow.

As with the standard business email, keep your e-newsletters short. Write a paragraph or two on a new product or promotion, include an image or two to illustrate the content, and, of course, provide contact information in case any of your recipients wants to follow up for purchase. Don't be afraid to use humor, but, again, keep it clean!

Send your e-newsletters regularly. In order to keep your customers engaged, you want to send your e-newsletters on a consistent basis—say, every Thursday, or every other Monday. This keeps your product or service in the eye of your public, and makes your customer base more likely to buy.

You can format your own e-newsletter using conventional email techniques, but there are also software programs and services (such as Constant Contact) that will help design your e-newsletter for you, insuring that the e-news you send is dynamic and attractive.

Be street smart; use e-newsletters to keep your customers interested and ready to buy!

■ PROSPECTING BY TELEPHONE

If ever there were a national sales pros' award show, it would definitely have to be named after Alexander Graham Bell. The telephone, invented by Bell, is still the greatest sales tool. Because of the telephone, sales pros can reach out and talk to another human being anywhere in the world—and on a personal level.

While email has its place, many sales pros have used it to the exclusion of the telephone. Not street smart sales pros. They know that the telephone is still an effective tool for reaching people. Instead of sitting around, hoping to get company-generated leads, these artful sales pros are constantly on the telephone, trying to make appointments to tell their story. There are some things that email just can't do: It can't explain complicated matters quickly, it can't gauge customer reactions as accurately, and it can't convey the warmth and sense of emotion as well as a phone call does. A live phone conversation can do a lot to advance the personal connection between you and your prospect. If the telephone does not play a large part in your sales program, read this section carefully. It will give you street smart tactics on how to maximize your telephone prospecting techniques.

Sound Enthusiastic

When using the telephone, you must be conscious of how you sound and the words that you use. A prospect whom you are calling for the first time to set up an appointment can only judge you by your voice. Your prospect cannot see you, your product, brochures, or any other aids that will help you on your face-to-face sales call. If she hears a sales pro who has a boring, monotonous voice and poor diction, she most likely will choose not to see you.

Street smart sales pros always sound enthusiastic when speaking to a prospect. Their enunciation is clear, so that they can be easily understood. These skillful sales pros choose their words carefully, trying to paint clear mental pictures of opportunity to their prospects. They get appointments because they create interest on the telephone.

Practice, Practice, Practice

Never ad-lib your telephone presentations, using different approaches each time you speak to a prospect. Your presentation on the telephone should be well-scripted. It should include a question or two that will engage your prospect in a short conversation. The word *convert* is associated with the word *conversation*. With conversation you have a better chance of converting your phone call into an appointment. In addition, you should be prepared to answer any objections that might come up. Role play with friends, relatives, or colleagues until you feel and sound natural and comfortable.

Remember the Goal

Your call should have a specific purpose in mind. You are not trying to sell your product or service on the telephone. Your only purpose is to get an appointment, nothing more. If a prospect asks you for information that could lead you to tell more, then you should use this response, "That's why I am calling, to set up an appointment to cover these types of things."

Prospects will try to find out how much your product or service will cost before seeing you. This can severely hurt your chances of getting an appointment, since they will be making their judgment strictly on price. Here is a street smart answer to such a question:

Sales pro: Before I answer your question on price, let me ask you a question. Leah, how much will you give me for my 1985 Pontiac?

Prospect: How can I say; I have to see it.

Sales pro: Exactly, Leah, and it is the same with my product. You have to see and hear what it can do for you.

Prospects will often ask you to send them brochures. For the most part, that is a kiss-off and a waste of your time. The street smart answer to this request is, "Justin, our brochure is 5'11" and weighs 185 pounds; which day is better, Monday or Wednesday, to drop it off?" If you do not come off as a smart aleck, it can be very effective. Often, your prospect will laugh and give you your appointment.

In order to have an effective prospecting program using the telephone, you must set up specific times to call each day. If you are not disciplined in your telephoning, it will become an ad hoc tool and eventually will not be used often enough to have any sustained value.

Be street smart; take advantage of Alexander Graham Bell's invention, and dial for dollars!

■ CANVASSING

Canvassing can be an effective way of prospecting if used wisely. I am not an advocate of getting up in the morning and knocking cold on doors. It's not a productive use of time. Utilizing the telephone, I believe, is a much wiser and more effective way of using your energies. But if you find yourself in an office building after finishing a sales call, stop in to the other offices and introduce yourself. At times, you may even get an opportunity to give a sales talk. If not, at least find out the name of the person whom you would like to see. Leave your card or brochure, indicating to the prospect's secretary that you will be following up with a telephone call to set up an appointment.

The important point is that you obtain the name of the individual to whom you need to speak, as well as his secretary's name. When calling back, it sometimes helps you to get through to the person you want to speak to by having the secretary's name. "Hello, Pat, is Mr. Brown in?" This gives the impression that you know the secretary as well as Mr. Brown. In some instances, even though he does not recognize your voice, he will put you through to Mr. Brown, not wanting to admit that he has forgotten who you are. This does not happen often, but as street smart sales pros, we take whatever edge we can gain!

■ DIRECT MAIL

Direct mail—sending brochures, letters, or clever attention-getters is another traditional method of prospecting for customers. The downside to this program is that, just as with email, people in business are besieged with all sorts of direct mail pieces. If your letter or mailing piece is not clever or different, you will not get the results. Your letter will get thrown out with tons of other junk mail pieces.

Street smart sales pros will handwrite the address on the envelope in order to personalize their material. Prospects are not so inclined to throw out a piece of mail without opening it if it is handwritten. Street smart sales pros will frequently write their introductory letter on stationery without a letterhead. This tactic is used to insure that the prospect will read at least the first line or two. Think about it: How often do you throw away a mailing piece right after you glance at the letterhead? If you use a mailing piece, make sure that the first sentence or two will catch your prospect's interest.

Street smart sales pros will often telephone the people to whom they have sent a direct mail piece. This approach definitely increases their prospecting results. After all, they are taking an aggressive approach, and are not just waiting for a potential customer to contact them. Direct mail should be used to supplement your prospecting methods. Do not rely solely on it to gain new leads.

■ SPECIAL PROMOTIONS

Trade and consumer shows offer excellent opportunities to gain leads. Trade shows are usually sponsored by the industry to which your company belongs. People who attend these shows are excited to see the advances and new products that have been developed during the year—your audience is already built in! To attract the attention of the people, companies spend a great deal of money on their display booths.

Many sales pros avoid working these shows because they usually require travel and long hours. If you are given the opportunity to work an industry show, do it. It is an excellent place to make contact with potential customers. You are far more likely to meet with success when calling up a person for an appointment if you have already met him face to face.

Consumer shows are slightly different. They are not industry based and are open to the general public. They can be antique shows, auto shows, home-improvement shows, flea markets, etc. Many different kinds of products and services are usually offered. What is important about these shows is that they usually draw a lot of people. And where there are people, there are potential customers. Search out these shows. Pick the ones that will benefit you the most.

When I first began selling recreational property, I built my own booth, featuring a few pictures of vacant property. On the counter, I had a huge pile of dirt with a sign over it saying, "For Sale." I set this display up in my local flea market. My colleagues said I was wasting my time. I knew better, and after I began making sales, my fellow sales pros did the same.

Be street smart, get out to the people. That's where the action is.

■ NEWSPAPERS

Street smart sales pros use newspapers to prospect. While their circulations may be declining, newspapers are still replete with valuable clues about prospects. City and local papers provide valuable information about people and companies. Newspapers report on who has been promoted. They reveal if a celebrity is moving into the area. This information can be invaluable to a sales pro selling insurance, home improvements, real estate, etc.

Look carefully at the job opening section—but for jobs, for additional leads. Newspapers run ads for companies looking to hire. Companies that hire are usually expanding, which may prove helpful to a sales pro who does recruiting, office sales, real estate, etc.

Read the paper with a prospecting eye; it is the street smart thing to do.

■ TURNOVER

At some time or another, all companies experience turnover in their sales department. When this occurs, what do you think the salespeople leave behind? Right—their customer lists. Don't let these lists sit idle. When salespeople leave your company, ask your sales manager if you can go through their files and see if you can develop business.

If a prospect informs you that he stopped doing business because he was not happy with the way he was handled, tell him that that is the exact reason you were assigned to his company—to provide him with the best service possible.

■ OLD CUSTOMERS

Street smart sales pros prospect by calling or emailing old clients. Most products have a natural life cycle, and it is your job to figure out when your prospect will be in the market again. If you sell cars, ask your customer at the time of purchase how often he purchases a new automobile. Make note of this information on your customer database.

Because products or services having long life cycles are infrequent or one-time sales, you can be remembered as your client's sole supplier by sending him a line from time to time and asking how your products are holding up. If he's willing, keep him in the loop by adding him to your e-news list! If there have been technical advances made on your product, your e-newsletter will inform your customers about them. It is human nature to want the newest and the best. By maintaining contact with your old clients, you insure that your product or service stays in their consciousness. When others ask him if he knows where to get a particular item, it will be you that he recommends.

Be street smart; don't always look for new faces. Some of the old ones might be very rewarding.

Consider This

The goal of all the tools that I have described is to get an individual to buy whatever it is you are selling. Street smart sales pros know that the more people they see, the better are their chances of earning those large commission checks. Don't cut down your chances by depending on your company to supply you with prospects. Go out and make it happen for yourself by employing these street smart prospecting tactics.

The following questions are designed to get you to prospect like a street smart sales pro. Read these questions, think about them carefully, and answer them on a sheet of paper.

1. What percentage of your day is set aside for prospecting?

2. What methods do you use to prospect for customers?

3. Currently, what type of prospecting produces the most leads for you?

4. Do you depend solely on company-generated leads? If so, why?

5. What type of prospecting do you think could be more effective with the type of product or service you represent?

6. What is the life cycle of your product?

7. Are you successful in obtaining referrals from clients? If not, why not?

8. Do you have a well-scripted telephone presentation? If not, why not?

Now that you have completed this chapter, you should realize that you do not have to depend solely on company-generated leads to see potential prospects. In fact, the less you depend on your company, the more you will earn. Street smart sales pros are successful because they are not satisfied with what their company can do for them with respect to leads. They are not content to sit back and hope that their company can supply them with sufficient leads to make a living. Street smart sales pros are looking to make much more than a living—they are looking to make a real life for themselves and their families.

If after reading all these prospecting techniques, you still find that you would not be comfortable prospecting, then close this book and give it to a friend who can use it. Selling may not be for you. However, if you are excited and enthusiastic about all the fantastic opportunities out there for you, then you have taken a major step towards becoming a street smart sales pro!

8

The Presentation

What is a sales presentation? This is a simple, straightforward question, yet most salespeople are not able to answer it accurately. A presentation is the complete sales package that is given to a prospect for the sole purpose of getting her to commit to purchase a product or service. It is the road map that gets you from point A to point B. The world is full of underachievers who believe that their sales presentations begin the moment they first meet their prospects and end when they either get a "Yes, I will do business with you," or a "No, I am not interested."

Street smart sales pros know that this is nonsense. These tactical sales pros are aware that their presentations begin way before they ever meet their prospects. And when they do meet their prospects, they do not base their sales talk on a bunch of ad-libbed razzle-dazzle. No way! These earners break down their presentations into component parts, and each part becomes an important element in making their sales calls successful.

The Elements of a Strong Presentation

There are three essential elements that go into developing a successful presentation. The first is *preparation*. Street smart sales pros learn as much as they can about their product, their competition, their customers, and their markets. As soon as the street smart sales pros become confident in this fact-finding process, they make sure that all their information is well organized so it can be used effectively. On many occasions, I have witnessed salespeople frantically looking for contracts, phone numbers, sales proposals, and other important items at critical moments in their presentations. Not very professional.

The sales pitch, the actual communication between you and your prospect, is the second essential element that goes into your presentation. During this time, you are trying to discover what your customer's needs are. This is accomplished by having a well-planned presentation that asks specific questions of your prospect. If your listening skills are where they should be, the answers will supply you with valuable customer information. As soon as your prospect's needs are established, your presentation will indicate to your prospect how she will benefit, and satisfy these needs with use of your product or service.

At some point during your sales call, you are bound to encounter customer objections. This affords you the opportunity to prepare answers to your prospect's objections in a logical, straightforward, convincing manner.

The third component of your presentation is *the close.* It should accomplish one of two things. It should indicate a decision on the part of your buyer to go or not to go with you, or it should establish a commitment for some future action, such as a follow-up appointment.

The street smart sales pro's roadmap is completed as soon as she is able to incorporate all these components into her sales presentation. Like a motorist on a journey, she will be guided from preparation to close by her sales presentation, directed how and where to go by the presentation's components. Meanwhile, she is free to anticipate any detours such as customer objections, questions, etc.

Underachievers are not successful because their presentations are poorly structured and ill-planned, which prohibits their picking up valuable clues and information necessary to successfully close their sales.

If on your sales calls you do not have a clear-cut understanding as to where you are going, it is time for you to develop a well-planned strategic presentation that will enable you to uncover the important clues about your prospect's needs, wants, or interests. Once that is accomplished, you will begin to make sale after sale. Read this chapter carefully; it will help you plot out a money-making street smart sales presentation.

Preparation

Does a boxer go into a ring without getting into condition? No! Does a surgeon operate without years of study? No! Does an actor go on stage without any rehearsal? No! Does the street smart sales pro go into a sales call without preparation? Absolutely not!

Like all champions, street smart sales pros prepare and practice their craft over and over again. They know there are no shortcuts to success. A salesperson who goes on a sales call poorly prepared will severely cut down her chances to earn those large commission checks. Street smart sales pros will not allow this to happen, and neither should you.

The section that follows will prove invaluable by helping you to prepare a well-planned presentation. Be street smart—start mapping out how and where you want to go; it will lead to big bucks!

■ KNOW WHAT YOU'RE SELLING

Street smart sales pros want to know their products inside and out— and then some. They are constantly trying to educate themselves with new information that will enable them to increase their product knowledge. Underachievers believe that product knowledge means being familiar with a few features of their products or services, and maybe having some buzzwords at hand in order to convince the prospect that they know what they are taking about. This is ridiculous.

You must know your product as if it were part of your body. When you are explaining a feature of your product to your prospect, it is best to assume that she knows very little about your product or service. In most cases, your prospect will indicate to you if she is familiar with the point you are trying to make.

Now that we have established the importance of product knowledge, I can see that you were just about to ask me what you should be looking to discover about your product or service. I'm glad you're eager to learn; let's get to it.

A good start in developing product knowledge is being well versed in the history of your product or service. If your company has made technical advances over the years, be able to talk about them in your presentation. Some of your sales may have been lost due to the fact that you were not aware of some of the achievements that your company has made over the years. These achievements could be in many different areas, such as manufacturing, packing, delivery, use of personnel, etc.

Perhaps your company started out in a small facility, like a basement or some other such humble place. Indicate to your prospect just how far your company has come. Prospects like to do business with growth companies. It gives them a feeling of security to know that your business will be around to service them in the future.

If your company happens to be second or third generation, tell your prospects that the owner has roots and cares about the day-to-day operation of his business. Emphasize that your boss is working extra hard to please her customers. She doesn't want anything to occur that will jeopardize a business started by her grandfather, grandmother, father, or mother. Talk about the values of past owners, and how these values were handed down from generation to generation. Sales talks that include these kinds of things help to promote trust, empathy, and a good rapport between you and your prospect.

In some instances, it might be beneficial for you to have a good understanding of what actually goes into the making of your product, especially if your company uses materials that go far beyond industry standards.

Where do you go if your company doesn't have this information readily available? This is another excellent question, and here is the answer. Talk to older employees; they often will be able to tell you about the good old days, when the company started in a little two-by-four office. A foreperson in the factory can provide you with all sorts of information that can help you on your sales calls. Vendors who sell to your company can be an excellent source of information, letting you know about the advances that they have made in the materials or procedures that they supply for your product. Other reps or salespeople can also give you a sense of company history. Try to locate old company brochures. Many times you can use them on a sales call, indicating to your prospect the progress that your company has achieved over the years. Last but not least, your boss can give you an excellent sense of history about the company. You will find that owners enjoy talking about their company's beginnings. The good old days, so to speak.

As a result of learning about new strengths of your products or services, you will be able to keep up a high level of enthusiasm. When you stop trying to learn about your products or services, you will become bored and burnt out. It is impossible to excite prospects to buy when you yourself are unenthusiastic.

By acquiring strong product knowledge, you as a representative of your company will develop the confidence needed to go after the larger and more difficult accounts. Underachievers are intimidated easily because they are not secure about what they are selling. They fear they will not have the knowledge to answer certain objections or questions. Prospects can sense when a sales pro is either nervous or unsure of herself, and prospects do not buy from sales pros who aren't confident about the product or service they are selling.

The more you know about your products or services, the better able you will be to indicate to your prospects all the benefits that they can expect to receive by purchasing. The Nobel Prize-winning scientist Albert Szent-Györgyi once said, "Discovery consists of seeing what everybody has seen and thinking what nobody has thought." That is exactly the way a street smart sales pro looks upon her products or services, trying to come up with new insights that no one else has considered.

Be street smart; do your homework, it will be well worth the effort.

■ KNOWING YOUR COMPETITION

Street smart sales pros are aware that having strong product knowledge is only half the battle; the other half is gaining as much information about their competition as possible. These savvy sales pros would never develop a presentation that did not take into consideration who and what they are up against. Only then can they be in a position to construct a sales presentation that will be able to convey the strength of their products or services without knocking their competition. One of the worst things that a sales pro can do is to overtly knock her competition. If you do such a thing, all it accomplishes is increased doubt in your customer's mind as to your own ethics, reliability, and the quality of your product or service.

In putting together their presentations, street smart sales pros try to get as much information as possible as to how and when their competitors will go about selling their products or services. If you are not aware, you just might be selling at a tremendous disadvantage. It is important to know if the people you are up against use giveaways, colorful brochures, consignments, etc. Common sense tells you that if you don't know, then how the heck can you plan a presentation that will beat your competition?

A good source of information is your prospects themselves. Your customer can specifically tell you what she likes or dislikes about the products or services she is using. In addition, some prospects will reveal if they are either satisfied or unhappy with the sales pro who is presently servicing them. Often, they will even go into the reasons why they are happy or unhappy. You may learn that a sales pro has become so confident about getting a prospect's business that she takes the prospect for granted. Instead of servicing the prospect face to face, she takes the impersonal route by using the telephone or emailing.

By doing some detective work, you will find out how often your competitor works her territory, and in some instances, you will learn the specific days that she visits her customers, which can be extremely helpful, especially if it is advantageous to you to be there first or last.

If it is possible, go out and buy your competitors' products. Read their brochures. If you're a service company, get your competitors' service contracts, guarantees, etc. See if you can unearth independent studies that will give you valuable information as to how your product or service does indeed stack up to your competition.

After you have compared and dissected your competitors' products, make a list of all the strengths and weaknesses that you perceive they have. Then make a list of all the strengths and weaknesses of your products or services, carefully analyzing how your products or services stack up against theirs. Without doing this exercise, you will never be able to arm yourself with enough information in order to handle product comparison, which I can assure you will be brought up by your prospects.

Be street smart—learn as much about your competitor as possible. If not, she just might take away the business you were counting on.

■ SECURING REFERRALS

There are two types of referrals that street smart sales pros use: the letter and the personal contact. In some cases, a referral letter can be one of the most important items you can have on your sales call. It indicates that a customer who has already used your product or service has not only been satisfied, but has been satisfied enough to sit down and write a letter recommending your product or service to others.

Amazingly, many salespeople are very lax or uncomfortable about asking their clients for these letters. Street smart sales pros realize that referral letters are too important not to be requested. They know that in most cases, if a client is happy with your product or service, she will be willing to write you a letter of recommendation. The street smart sales pro is not afraid to ask, because if a client is not happy enough to write her a letter, she wants to know the reason why. Many times, after she has straightened out a problem for a prospect, she then will be able to secure a recommendation letter.

The best time to ask for a referral letter is as soon as possible after your product or service has been used. At that point, your prospect will have the most enthusiasm for you and your products or services.

In addition to getting your own letters of recommendation, ask other salespeople if they can share with you their letters that indicate client satisfaction with your products or services. The more testimonials you have about your company, the more secure a prospect will feel in purchasing your products or services.

The second type of referral requires a solid relationship with an existing client. When a customer asks, "How do I know if your product (or service) is good?", letters may not always work. Being able to provide them with the name and number of another client to call can make a crucial difference. Since you are the best judge as to whom to call, always get permission from your existing account in order to use her as a reference—and call or email her in advance to inform her that she may be getting a call from one of your potential customers. If you are new on the job, ask your boss or another sales rep to provide you with a reference to use.

Be street smart; get others to help you sell your wares. Remember, there is strength in numbers.

■ RECORD KEEPING

Street smart sales pros know the importance of keeping good records. All their customer information and research involving product knowledge and competitors would not be worth very much if these pros forgot, misplaced, or simply did not bother to write down what they had discovered. Composing a presentation from memory leads to too many important omissions.

All the records of the street smart sales pro are put into an electronic database that can be pulled up on site at an office computer or remotely on a lap top, tablet, or smartphone. These thorough sales pros know that it is just as important to have their records as complete and well organized as possible, allowing them to refer to any data that might be helpful in preparing their presentation. Besides the usual information, the database should also include notes on past conversations that you might have had with your prospect, as well as the reasons why you think you were or were not able to sell to her in the past. If your prospect has already bought, indicate on her file what she purchased.

You may think this is corny, and it is, but it works. Whenever a prospect becomes a customer of mine, I ask her for her birthday. Not only do I add it to my database, but I also set up a monthly calendar that has reminders for all my clients' birthdays. When I'm preparing to see a client, I look up her birthday. If it should happen that it is coming up shortly, I congratulate her during my presentation. You will see how effective it will be in establishing rapport between the two of you.

Many prospects inquisitively ask why, and here is my street smart answer:

Lisa, I send everyone in my family a birthday card. My clients are like family to me, and they get cards just like my kids, aunts and uncles, and brothers and sisters.

If there is any other pertinent information that you feel belongs in your database, include it. The more information that you have when going into a sales call, the better your chances of completing the sale. Don't count on your memory for your record keeping—be organized, be street smart, leave nothing to chance.

■ STAY IN TOUCH

There you are—at the right office, at the appropriate time—and the secretary says, "Sorry, but I called your office two hours ago to cancel today's appointment." Or, you make it back to your office at the end of the day and look down at your desk to see a note saying, "Call back hot prospect before 1 PM!!" Or, your biggest customer has left five voice messages for you to call him immediately, if not sooner. Bad timing? No. What we have here is a failure to communicate.

The street smart sales pro knows she must make herself accessible. If a customer needs to reschedule your appointment, if a hot lead comes in and needs immediate follow-up, if a question arises that only you can answer, the street smart sales pro will know. You have to make it your business—and that's what it amounts to, business—to be in touch with your office and your customers at all times. And yet, there are salespeople who don't make it a priority to always be in constant contact with their office or their clients.

Where only a decade ago, we were subject to cell phones with limited ranges, beepers, paging services, fax machines, and pay phones, today we live in a world that makes instant communication not only possible, but mandatory. Technology has made it unthinkable that a business connection could ever be lost: We have smartphones, redirected phone calls, laptops, tablets, and video conferencing, to mention just a few of the devices to which the sales pro has access. Make use of these assets! The street smart sales pro knows that a missed phone call or a delayed response to an email is a missed business opportunity. She makes it her priority to stay on top of her communications. Some street smart sales pros even keep separate phones for business and pleasure, so as to insure that they never miss out on a call.

By making sure your support people and clients always know how to reach you, you will avoid the pitfalls of missed messages or, worse, missed opportunities.

■ CLOTHES SELECTION

Street smart sales pros know the importance of dress, and they select their clothes very carefully before they go out on sales calls. They are aware that when a prospect decides to buy, her decision is based on the total package, and the sales pro is part of that total package. Many sales have been lost because the image projected by a salesperson's clothes has not been looked upon favorably by her prospect.

There is an old expression, "It is better to be overdressed than underdressed." For our male sales pros, I recommend that you always wear a shirt, a tie, and a suit. If you have to go on a job site with a client, you can always bring some protective clothing. Sales pros who wear casual clothes will not project the professional image that they want. Even if your prospect greets you in cutoffs, he will take notice of your professional look.

For male sales pros, I recommend the following dress:

- *Black Socks.* Colored socks can be distracting. They do not project a professional image; your outfit should bring the prospect's focus to your face, not your feet.

- *Navy Suit.* As you will learn later on, navy is a power color. Choose a good-quality fabric, preferably wool, and select a classic cut—a single-breasted, notched lapel, 2- or 3-buttoned jacket with a single back vent, and regular flap pockets. Your jacket should have at least as many cuff buttons as it has front buttons. Make sure you visit a tailor in order to have the suit properly fit to your specific dimensions, as an ill-fitting suit does you no favors. Even if you have just one suit—make it count!

- *White Shirt.* White projects a clean-cut, honest image. Your shirt should be cotton, and well-pressed; make sure that your shirt is wrinkle free. All your buttons should be buttoned.

- *Silk Tie.* Wear a silk tie of a conservative, understated color or pattern.

Your tie should not be louder than your sales pitch! Learn how to tie a correct four-in-hand or half-Windsor knot; nothing is less professional than a poorly arranged tie. And make sure the length is correct; the tip of your tie should hit at your beltline or slightly above.

- *Black Shoes.* As with colored socks, colored shoes can be very distracting. Wear good-quality black shoes, and make sure they are made of leather. Plain Oxfords are your best bet. Make sure your shoes are shined, not scuffed. This indicates that you take care of your appearance (and, by extension, of your customers).

- *Overcoat.* Cashmere is the best; wool is fine. Ski jackets and three-quarter coats do not project a successful, professional image; choose a full-length coat instead.

- *Briefcase.* Leather is the only way to go. Vinyl, cloth, or supermarket bags are not acceptable.

- *Jewelry.* A nice watch is about as much jewelry as the male sales pro should wear. Avoid the "aurous syndrome"—curvature of the neck due to the excessive weight of gold chains.

Saleswomen are also expected to apply standards of decorum to their business attire. While women are no longer expected to dress like Puritans in order to be taken seriously, cleavage and skin-tight skirts have no place on a sales call. Dress conservatively, and use common sense and good taste to avoid standing out in a bad way! Women do have more leeway in the colors that they choose to incorporate into their clothes. They can wear prints as long as their clothes do not take away from the professional image that they are trying to establish.

For saleswomen, I recommend the following dress:

- *Suits.* Business suits indicate just that—you are there to do business. Navy and gray will give you the corporate image that you desire, and wool or wool blend materials will project quality. While the business community has historically preferred the skirt suit, pantsuits are increasingly deemed acceptable, made popular by such powerful women as Nancy Reagan and Hillary Clinton. As with any suit, make sure yours fits properly; visit a tailor to have your suit tweaked to your specific dimensions.

- *Skirt.* Choose a skirt that allows you to sit comfortably in front of a prospect without being concerned that you have too much leg showing. Skirts should be just above, or slightly below, knee level.

- *Blazer.* If you don't feel comfortable in a formal suit, consider pairing a blazer or fitted jacket with your skirt. Blazers should be of good-quality material (wool, silk, or another fine fabric) and provide some structure to your look. Again, go for dark colors or neutral for that corporate look.

- *Shoes.* Leave the stilettos, platforms, and flip-flops at home. Instead, opt for low heels (two inches or shorter) or flats if you absolutely can't wear heels. No loud colors or patterns, and no patent leather; your shoes shouldn't do the talking for you. Avoid sling-backs and open-toed shoes; these have historically been considered unacceptable for the workplace.

- *Stockings.* Stockings that most closely match the color of your skin are preferred. Avoid colored, patterned, or textured hose, and don't go bare-legged.

- *Handbags.* As with the men's accessories, ladies' handbags and briefcases should be leather; this will project the idea that the person knows quality.

- *Jewelry.* Keep your accessories to a minimum; any jewelry you wear should be tasteful and conservative. No bright colors, and nothing that jangles when you move!

- *Perfume.* If you must wear a scent, choose one that is unobtrusive and apply it sparingly. You don't want your perfume to announce your presence before you even see a prospect!

- *Makeup.* Keep yours to a minimum; the goal is to sell, not seduce.

For all salespeople, if your clothes look as if you have eaten too many chili dogs, bursting at the seams, bring them to a tailor; if the tailor can't fix them, buy a new suit. Remember, your hair and nails are part of the total package; it is essential that you be well groomed.

The street smart sales pro knows that a conservative style is the best style, at least where business success is concerned. Study after study indicates that the vast majority of the most successful sales representative dress in the fashion I have outlined above. There may always be exceptions to the rule; experience will quickly indicate if you are that exception. As they say, dress not for the job you have, but for the job you want to have. Invest in at least one high-quality outfit and make it count!

My advice to all is simple: Be street smart—dress like a winner, even if you have only one outfit.

■ YOUR SALES DELIVERY

Street smart sales pros understand that it is not always what you say to a client that makes a positive impression but, in many instances, how you make that statement. A sales rep trying to convey her empathy to a client who is having difficulties will only hurt her chances of success if she does not convey a sincere feeling of compassion on her part. Prospects do not like to do business with salespeople who they feel are a bunch of phonies.

There will be points during your presentation when you may have to express confidence, compassion, concern, etc., which will help you to develop a strong bond with your prospect.

In order to insure that your sales delivery conveys the messages that are needed, the following steps should be taken. If your sales call only requires you to give a talk, make certain that you script your speech before making it. By preparing it ahead of time, you then have the opportunity to commit it to memory. Once it is memorized, you can practice and refine your presentation, creating the moods that are needed. You can show empathy, humor, or whatever other emotion is called for.

Speak in a confident tone, but be careful not to talk too quickly, or you will give the impression that you are nervous. Fear of speaking can play havoc with how quickly you speak. If you have to slow down, breathe deeply; it will help you relax.

I don't want to give you too much to remember, but you also have to concentrate on not speaking too slowly; this can give the impression that you are unsure of yourself, or even worse, that you believe your prospect is not smart enough to follow what you are saying. If you have rehearsed enough and keep your enthusiasm up, you should not have any trouble.

If, on the other hand, you are going to do a PowerPoint presentation or demonstrate a product, do a trial run for friends or colleagues that allows you to do a step-by-step analysis of what you are going to show off in your demonstration,. Ask them if you kept their interest up. There are very few things that are more boring than a poor demonstration.

A good practice exercise is to rehearse in front of a friend, relative, or colleague, having her role play as if she were a prospect. See if she can tell the moods that you are trying to convey. Ask her if what you are saying makes sense and is easily understood. Practice pacing yourself with clear, crisp enunciation, changing pitch and tone every so often to avoid becoming too monotonous. Don't be afraid to be animated; use your arms to make significant points. Afterwards, have your listener as well as yourself critique your performance, making any additional changes that are required. Do this exercise over and over again until what you say feels and sounds completely natural and comfortable.

Underachievers who are not prepared, and put off practicing as if it is some kind of punishment, can sound awkward, stiff, and confusing. Many times they even leave out important information that could be critical in making the sale.

As in other fields, champions in sales do not reach greatness without sacrifice and practice. Be street smart—practice, practice, practice; it will lead to commissions, commissions, commissions!

The Pitch

Your sales pitch, the actual face-to-face meeting with your prospect, is what all your work, preparation, and rehearsal are for. Street smart sales pros are keenly aware that the sales pitch is their opportunity to make it happen. If you present yourself poorly the first time, the chances of getting another opportunity are slim. These superb sales pros know that if they perform in a professional, logical manner, with a presentation that meets the needs of their prospect, their chances of earning those large commission checks are excellent, and that's the bottom line!

■ THE FIRST IMPRESSION

Think about it. When you first meet someone, how long does it take you to decide if you like that individual or not? I suspect not very long. At times, I don't even have to speak to a person before I determine whether or not I am going to like him. An arrogant gesture can turn me off, and afterwards I try my best to avoid that person. On the other hand, I have found myself drawn towards an individual who merely displayed a nice warm smile.

Your prospects are also prone to making quick judgments about you. It does not take them very long to develop an impression of you. Do not give them any help in formulating a negative one.

Wear your best outfit, and walk in with confidence: head up, shoulders back, with a warm smile on your face. Do not start out by making weak statements such as:

- "I won't be taking too much of your time."

- "Thank you for giving me some time today."

Many sales pros make the following typical, weak statement when their prospects either interrupt or stop their presentations to concentrate on some other matter:

- "Take your time; I have all day."

Always be positive; remember you are there to help your prospect, you are an asset. Don't tell your prospect that you have all day. People who have all day do not have much to offer. You must make your prospect feel that you have an opportunity for him. Introduce yourself, your company, and your product in an upbeat, confident manner. Never apologize for being there. And for God's sake, be on time.

■ HOW TO ADDRESS YOUR PROSPECT

"Hi Claire, I'm Charlie. How are ya?" Sounds friendly enough, but chances are that Claire is not interested in making new friends in the middle of her work day. For that reason, when meeting your prospect for the first time, take the utmost care and greet her with respect—and make sure to get her name right. Always address her formally:

- "I'm pleased to meet you, Dr. Forster."
- "Ms. Chandler, I'm so glad we could talk."

Since you don't know how informal or formal your new prospect is, you should never address her by her first name unless you are given a verbal indication to do so. There are some customers who prefer to be addressed by their title, such as "doctor" or "professor," and surname; you may already have a client or two who will always be known as "Mr. Bryant" or "Mrs. Jackson." When in doubt, stay formal.

Chances are good, however, that your prospect will immediately tell you to address her by her given name—"Charlie, please call me Claire." This is ideal; you want to establish a friendly, casual rapport with your client as quickly as possible, and getting onto a first-name basis can be the key to this process. Doing so will greatly improve the likelihood of your creating a more congenial environment. Prospects are more willing to buy from people with whom they feel comfortable.

If no invitation is given, often you will be able to ease into a first-name basis over time, as your client gets to know you better, through several phone calls or meetings. Don't force the issue; allow the client to dictate the terms of engagement, but make sure your own manner of speaking helps to initiate a closer rapport. Sometimes your client is actually waiting for you to break the ice; if given the opportunity, you can be the one to initiate the use of your given names by telling *her*, "Please, call me Charlie."

Be street smart—listen to your clients, and talk to them at the level of formality they prefer!

■ NEED-SATISFACTION

Street smart sales pros are aware that their customers' needs are the focal point of any sales transaction. No one, and I mean no one, buys a product or service unless she thinks that it is going to satisfy one of her particular needs. Simply put, a *need* is something that your prospect wants. It can be a tangible item or an intangible desire.

As a sales pro, you must be able to communicate to your prospect how the benefits of your product or service will satisfy her needs. Your presentation has to be structured in such a fashion that it encourages your prospect to communicate to you what her needs are. And that is the key: having a two-way dialogue between you and your customer.

Knowing this, street smart sales pros have in their selling bags a list of probing questions that they can ask their prospects in order to gain valuable information about their clients' needs, wants, or interests. These questions are prepared long before they even meet their prospect; they are built into the presentation. Even though most of the questions may never be used, they are still made available. In later chapters we will discuss in greater detail the importance of asking questions and listening to your prospect's answers. Below are examples of good questions that can give you an idea as to how to discover customer needs:

- "What are the barriers that are preventing you from achieving great success?"

- "How is competition hurting you in the marketplace?"

- "If you were to retain a company like mine, what would you want it to do for you?"

- "What would you like to see as the future of your company?"

Pay careful attention to the way your prospect answers your questions. A gesture or a tone of voice can give you additional clues as to her needs. See Chapter 9, "Subliminal Selling," which tells you what to look for and how to interpret your prospect's body language.

Be street smart—discover what your prospect's needs are; this will dramatically help you in satisfying yours!

■ FEATURE-SATISFACTION

As soon as the street smart sales pro establishes customer needs, she will indicate to her prospect all the unique features of her products or services that can satisfy the prospect as well as her company's needs.

A *feature* is any specific characteristic of your product or service that can be translated into benefits for your prospect.

In order for you to be able to translate the features of your products or services into customer benefits, it is essential that you have a thorough understanding of your products or services. That includes special achievements, unique manufacturing techniques, strengths, material advantages, and history of your products, services, and company.

It is critical that your presentation convey these unique features to your prospect so that she can truly see and understand how she will benefit by deciding to purchase your products or services.

Be street smart—know the important features of your products; it just might make you unique!

■ BENEFIT-SATISFACTION

Street smart sales pros are aware that the key to selling is the process of satisfying customer needs with product benefits. A *benefit* is any perceived value of your products or services that can satisfy a prospect's needs. Product benefits are the link between your products' or services' features and your customer's needs.

Underachievers are unable to close their share of sales because they do not sufficiently indicate to their prospects how their products or services will benefit them. As a result, their prospects are not confident about making the decision to purchase. That is why many of the underachievers cannot overcome the "I want to think it over" objection. If their prospects were clearly shown how they could benefit from the underachievers' products or services, many of the "I want to think it over" prospects would purchase right away.

Be street smart—indicate clearly how your products or services will benefit your prospect. Once you do, you will reap the rewards.

■ HOW TO USE NEED-, FEATURE-,
AND BENEFIT-SATISFACTION SELLING

Street smart sales pros use need-, feature- and benefit-satisfaction selling to close a high percentage of their prospects. By using the technique of asking questions, they are able to uncover their prospects' needs. Once these needs are established, they are then able to indicate to their prospects all the unique features of their products or services that will benefit them as well as their companies. The following example will illustrate this point:

Customer: I get a lot of returns due to widget corrosion. (*Need is established. A widget that will not corrode is needed.*)

Sales pro: My widget has been specially treated with chrome-plated latches. (*Chrome-plated latches represent the special feature of the product.*)

Sales pro: As a result, you will no longer get returns due to widget corrosion. (*The customer will benefit by not getting any returns due to corrosion.*)

Upon hearing a customer need, be sure not to make the mistake of going right into closing and stating a benefit of your products or services without emphasizing any of the features. The following examples will illustrate this point:

Customer: Sales are way down. I'm not making any money.

Sales pro: I can assure you that if you give our company a chance, you will make money.

By closing in this fashion, without using feature support of her statement, the sales pro is asking the customer to take her word at face value. The correct way to indicate to the customer that she will benefit by the product would be:

Sales pro: Because our machine has a Fibulating Microprocessor (*unique feature*) it will produce your goods five times faster, dramatically cutting your manufacturing costs. As a result you will be able to drop your prices, which will enable you to increase your sales. (*Customer benefit is established.*)

In summary, selling is the process of satisfying customer needs with product benefits. Your product benefits connect your product features and your customer needs. When a prospect feels trust and rapport with you, and perceives that your products or services will benefit her, she will most likely make a positive decision to purchase.

Be street smart—translate the features of your products or services into benefits for her; this will benefit you as well by meeting your large commission needs.

■ ANTICIPATING OBJECTIONS

The third key component in your presentation is your ability to anticipate and handle your prospect's objections. No matter how thorough your presentation is, at some point your prospect is going to throw an objection out to you, and the way that you handle it can make the difference between making the sale or not.

The following exercise will help you anticipate what some of your prospect's objections might be. Thoroughly go over the presentation that you have written out. When you get to a point where you believe there might be a customer objection, write it down on a piece of paper. After this, do your presentation for a friend or colleague, asking her to give you any objections that might come into her mind. When you have finished these exercises, continue to practice and work on solutions to these problems. Practice your answers on your friends, getting additional input. You may not always be able to come up with answers that will satisfy all your customers, but at least you will sound professional and confident. The worst thing that you can do is to fumble for answers, which will only add to your prospect's concerns.

Be street smart—don't be caught off guard; try to anticipate as many of your prospect's objections as possible.

■ OVERCOMING OBJECTIONS

The ability to anticipate objections is important, but not nearly as important as developing the skills to overcome your prospect's concerns. No matter how much you prepare and try to list everything that a client could possibly question, there will still be occasions when a prospect will throw out an objection that you had not considered.

Don't panic—the street smart sales pro has everything under control. In Chapter 11, "Handling Objections," you will find means for overcoming client objections. These tactics will give you enormous confidence. No longer will you fear objections by your prospects; rather, you will welcome them. You will learn that customer objections indicate interest, and interest is all you should hope for when going on a sales call.

Be street smart—read and study the chapter on objections; it will help you overcome any of your concerns.

The Close

Closing is the last element in your presentation. It is the point at which you ask your prospect for some action. Street smart sales pros are keenly aware that a strong presentation will give them an opportunity to ask their clients for commitment at different points during their sales talk. These proficient sales pros know that if they wait until the very end of their presentation to ask for the order, they are putting too much pressure on the decision-making capabilities of their clients. Street smart sales pros use the trial close as a way to ask for the order at various times during their sales calls.

Trial closes give you indications as to how positive or negative your prospect may be at certain points in your presentation. They allow you as a sales pro to test the waters. A trial close gives you the flexibility to ask for the order without risking a halt to your presentation.

In Chapter 12, "Closing," you will find many additional tactics that you can use in order to get customer commitment. Study and incorporate them into your presentation. Role play with friends until you become comfortable and familiar with these techniques. The better you become at closing, the more sales and commissions you will make, which is the street smart bottom line!

Making Adjustments

Street smart sales pros know that part of being prepared is to expect the unexpected. These savvy sales pros understand that if they lose their composure or allow a prospect or situation to intimidate them, all chances for them to make a sale are most probably lost.

Read this section carefully and see how the street smart sales pro handles some of these out-of-the-ordinary situations.

■ SON-OF-A-BITCH PROSPECT

It is unfortunate when we come across a prospect who is rude, obnoxious, and arrogant—a real son-of-a-bitch. When a street smart sales pro comes across this kind of client, she does not allow the client's actions to destroy her motivation or self-image. She realizes that she has not done or thought about doing something that warrants this type of behavior. Yes, she is there to make a sale, which in effect should also benefit her prospect. But neither she nor any other salesperson is paid to take abuse. If a street smart sales pro feels as if she is being abused, she handles it in this manner:

> Alan, I sense by the way you are speaking to me that you do not like me. Did I do anything to offend you?

Most often, when you address a client in this direct manner, he will be taken by surprise. Like all bullies, when stood up to, he probably will back down and apologize for his behavior. On the other hand, if he looks at you and answers you in an abusive fashion, tell him in a nice way where he can stick it, and that you think too much of yourself and your company to allow this abuse to happen. You probably won't make the sale; but at least he will respect you. And more importantly, you will respect yourself.

Sometimes a son-of-a-bitch is not a son-of-a-bitch. He might tell you that you indeed said something that upset him. If his claims are legitimate, don't make excuses. Apologize; try to right the situation.

■ TIME CUT DOWN

Just as you are about to begin your presentation, your prospect announces that, instead of an hour, she can only give you ten minutes. Don't make the mistake of trying to rush your sales call, hoping to be able to cover sufficient material in order to close the sale. More often than not, you will not have the time to make the impression needed.

Instead, inform your prospect that what you have to tell her is far too important to rush through. This gives her a sense of urgency to see you again. Tell her that you understand that emergencies come up, and that it would be far better to reschedule than not be able to give her the information that she needs. Not only have you given her urgency to see you again; but, in addition, you have also shown empathy for her situation. This helps to build rapport between the two of you. It can only help you the next time you see her. Remember, before you leave, make sure you get a new date and time for the appointment.

In this case, it is better to put off till tomorrow what you would have to rush through today!

■ CONTINUED INTERRUPTIONS

There you are, trying to give a professional presentation, and for the past ten minutes your sales call has constantly been interrupted by secretaries, phone calls, or what have you. As a result of this, you are finding it difficult to concentrate. And you are aware that if you are having problems concentrating, there is an excellent chance that your prospect is not grasping anything you are saying. Street smart sales pros know that if this is the case they have to stop their presentation and say:

> Iris, I know I cannot convey the importance of my product or service to you because I am finding it difficult to concentrate on the important points due to all the interruptions. Why don't we take a break so you can catch up on what you have to do; and then could you please hold your calls until we have finished? This way, you will be able to make a wise decision about my product or service.

If your prospect says it is impossible to hold back the interruptions, take this street smart approach:

Sales pro: What time do you get into the office in the morning?

Prospect: 7 AM.

Sales pro: How about meeting me at 6:30, I'll bring the bagels and coffee, and we can talk in peace and quiet. (You can also use this tactic after hours if she is more of a night person. If she leaves the office at 6, meet her after closing.) I know you will benefit, because if we continue at this rate, you will not be able to get all the information that you need.

This approach shows that you care enough about her and her company to make the extra effort to come early or work late in order to accommodate her. Most prospects will appreciate this approach and agree to this arrangement.

■ CLIENT ASKS YOU TO COMPROMISE YOUR PRINCIPLES

There might be times when you are asked to compromise your principles. It could come in the form of payoffs to purchasing agents, or getting your hands on unrealistic amounts of samples in order to buy an order.

I can tell you that the sales obtained through unethical practices are not worth the business. It will always come back to haunt you. A buyer whom you pay off owns you. And like the blackmailer who never gets enough, that buyer will continually up her demands, to the point where it will become impossible to do business with her anyway.

If another prospect learns about certain favorable treatment, and she will, it most definitely will affect you with respect to getting her business. And who knows whom she will tell?

Inform your prospect that your reputation, as well as your company's, is everything. Ask her if she would be comfortable doing business with someone who is not trustworthy. Better yet, ask her how comfortable she would feel if she knew that someone working for her would compromise her company. Ease the tension by informing her that it would be your pleasure to have dinner with her or even take her to a show or sporting event. But you know that your company has made it a practice to give clients quality, service, and integrity, and isn't she happy that they have chosen to do that?

If she has an ounce of integrity, you will have made your point in a professional manner and should be able to get some business. On the other hand, if she doesn't have an ounce of integrity, you will get absolutely nothing. But be grateful; in the long run you will come out far ahead.

In summary, street smart sales pros are quick on their feet. They know that making adjustments is part of their presentation.

Advantages of a Well-Planned Presentation

Many sales reps avoid using a well-planned presentation because they are afraid that it will turn them into robots, making them sound stiff and void of personality. Street smart sales pros know that just ain't so; lack of planning is a total cop-out. The reason so many salespeople avoid a structured, well-planned presentation is due to the fact that they do not have the discipline to develop one.

The fact of the matter is, a structured, well-planned presentation gives you greater flexibility than one that is based on ad-lib, off-the-cuff remarks. By thoroughly preparing yourself, you will be able to address and emphasize any area that your prospect might show interest in, not just the areas that you might feel most comfortable with.

If a prospect shows interest in long-term stability, you will be prepared to discuss how your products or services will provide her with long-term stability. If she shows interest in economy, you will be prepared to discuss how your products or services will provide him with added economy, and so on and so on.

By having a well-planned presentation, you will always feel that you are in control of the sales call; you will be secure in your facts, knowing exactly where you want to go. This helps you to develop enormous confidence in your abilities as a sales pro, confidence that will help you make a favorable impression on your prospects. Prospects feel secure working with individuals who are confident; and when they feel secure, they buy!

A well-planned presentation insures that you will not forget to talk about important facets of your products or services.

Many times, underachievers conducting off-the-cuff sales calls leave out pertinent information, which causes them to lose their sales. In addition, because much of their sales presentation is ad-libbed, their pitch tends to jump around, repeating facts that can become confusing to their prospects. Prospects do not buy when they are confused.

By having a well-planned presentation, street smart sales pros are able to concentrate on their prospects' thoughts and gestures. They do not have to worry about what their next thought should be. As we will discuss in further detail in later chapters, an important aspect of becoming a street smart sales pro is to be able to pick up valuable clues from your prospects, such as gestures, tone of voice, etc., which will help you enormously on your sales calls. A sales pro who has to concentrate on what she has to say cannot possibly pay full attention to the actions or thoughts of others.

Be street smart—don't get lost on your sales calls; develop a well-planned map. It will lead to much success.

Out-of-Office Settings

Most sales visits occur in a cubicle, office, workshop, or conference room. The overall information in this chapter relates well to these standard business environments. However, the street smart sales pros know that sometimes these business settings are not conducive to establishing a relationship or giving a presentation. Sometimes, it takes an out-of-office setting to go for the gold. Over the years, I have closed many sales on the golf course and in restaurants. Both have their own unique features that should always be kept in mind. There are also other venues and offers to consider, as you will see.

■ THE RESTAURANT

Restaurants can be excellent places to conduct business. They should be used for either lunch or dinner appointments. You can schedule meetings for breakfast, but only after you have established a reasonable relationship and closed the deal. A breakfast meeting leaves open the possibility that your prospect is still suffering from a hangover, a poor night's sleep, or a fight with her spouse. By lunch or dinner time, prospects are more likely to be caught up in their work day.

Too many times, a sales rep will choose a popular restaurant to impress the client. This can be a bad choice for many reasons. If the restaurant is popular, it can be packed with people sitting in chairs butted against one another. This is less than ideal, as you want to be able to have an intimate conversation with your client—not with the family of four sitting next to you. In addition, it can also be incredibly noisy, forcing your intimate conversation to become a shouting match, in which all you can do is yell at your client, hoping he will hear you. Then, of course, there is the potential for a long wait before being seated—even if you've already made a reservation. Any kind of wait is a distraction that delays or prevents your client from focusing on the deal.

As we discuss later, it is important to keep your client's company policies in mind when choosing a dining location. If your client is not allowed to accept meals from a salesperson and is thus expected to pay for herself, don't choose the ritziest, most expensive place in town. But don't settle for the company cafeteria, either—you want to set up shop in a special environment where your client can relax and enjoy herself, away from his daily environment and coworkers. Instead, find a place with good, affordable food and service—your prospect will appreciate your thoughtfulness.

As you can see, the place you choose can be crucial. If you are going to select a restaurant to go to, you need to consider the following factors:

- Is the restaurant noisy during its peak hours?

- Are the tables separated enough to provide some level of privacy?

- Does the restaurant take reservations, or must the host be tipped in order for you to get seated?

- Does the restaurant offer live entertainment during dinner hours?

- What type of food does the prospect like?

If you are going to ask your prospects out for a meal, you should always ask what type of food they prefer, or if they have a favorite restaurant whose noise level would be conducive to conversation. Normally, they know the places near their office, and understand that you'd like to go to a place in which you can carry on a business transaction. If they do not, don't press the issue. You need to find a place to go. Online restaurant review sites will help you find good options in your client's vicinity; most of these sites also discuss noise levels in their listings. If you are unfamiliar with the spot, you should definitely call ahead of time—not only to make a reservation, but also to get more information about the venue. If you are in any doubt as to the suitability of the restaurant, you might take the additional step of checking out the restaurant ahead of time.

On one occasion, I thought I had selected a restaurant that met all of my requirements for a dinner meeting. Unfortunately, though, I hadn't thought to ask about live music. As we sat down, a singer arrived, settled down behind a synthesizer, and began to perform several sets of Billy Joel's greatest hits. Now, don't get me wrong, I like Billy Joel—but not when played during one of my presentations!

This is why it's important to know your venue. By making sure you have some control over the restaurant that is selected, you can avoid uncomfortable environments, and create an enjoyable and relaxing moment to open up an account. Once you find a good place, put your customer at ease by discussing his family, interests, hobbies, and other personal matters. The goal is to build your rapport with the client; casual conversation will set the stage for more serious business talk once your client has warmed to you.

■ THE GOLF COURSE

For many people, the golf course is a perfect place to do business. They get a great deal of pleasure out of playing the game, they like getting away from the office, and they enjoy the camaraderie. Golf is a great way to bond. With that said, there are several issues to consider when asking out a prospect to play a full round.

First and probably most important: do you play? Never ask a prospect out if you are not a decent player. You can single-handedly turn the time you spend on the green with your prospect into a day of hell. Unless your prospect is as bad as you are, you must first learn how to play the game before you ask a possible client to play.

Normally, if you are doing the asking, you are also responsible for selecting the golfing range to play at. If you belong to a club, you invite your prospect to play there. If there are highly ranked public golf ranges nearby, you might set up a reservation there. Or if you have a friend who belongs to a private club, see if you can arrange to play at that club.

Once you get to the golfing course, keep the conversation casual at first. Be prepared to discuss his family and ask about his other hobbies, interests, or favorite golfing ranges. Try to discover common ground, and use it as a foundation from which to start discussing business.

The idea is very simple. The golf course allows you to build a friendly relationship with a client, making him more receptive to both you and your business. You are taking a golfer out to enjoy one of life's greatest pleasures; you may lose a game or two, but you may very well win over a new customer.

■ SPORTING EVENTS, PLAYS, AND CONCERTS

Many sales organizations have access to sporting events and other entertainments; either they buy season tickets or they buy tickets as needed. It is relatively easy to gauge just how enthusiastic a prospect might be about attending an event. Once the level of a prospect's interest becomes clear, sales pros know how and when to use those tickets to their full advantage.

While all potential sales opportunities should be considered important, in cold hard terms, the use of tickets should be weighted against the amount of business that can be derived out of a sale. When a potential sale is particularly big or valuable—say, there's an opportunity for repeat sales—the sales pro knows that offering concert or sports tickets to a prospect can make that prospect feel very positive or receptive towards a sales pitch. Don't ruin that mood by trying to make the sale at the game or concert; this puts unpleasant pressure on an otherwise enjoyable situation, and would be considered tacky to boot. In fact, while some reps insist on coming along to events, I advise you to take a hands-off approach. Don't go; instead, let your client attend with a companion of her own choosing. You want to create a sense of good will, not obligation. Always offer two tickets, at a minimum; your generosity will be appreciated.

The only exception to this rule is when the game is a playoff of any sort; you should definitely attend, and make a point of allowing your client to come with you. Your client will probably jump at the chance to go, regardless of the company, thus giving you a great opportunity to build your relationship with her. And, of course, because playoff tickets are expensive and hard to obtain, you'll be able to show your client just how much you appreciate her business.

These kinds of events go a long way towards solidifying a relationship between you and your prospects. Be street smart; use event tickets to your advantage!

■ KNOW THE RULES

Over the last decade, many businesses have instituted very specific
rules about allowing their buyers to accept meals, event tickets, or other
perks from salespeople. When selling to large firms, you must always
learn their rules about entertaining their buyers. In most circumstances,
these policies are posted on the companies' websites. If you cannot find
these rules, simply ask the buyer if it's against the company's policy to
take them out for meals. In many cases where restrictions are set up,
buyers are allowed to go out with sales reps as long as they pay for
their own meals. You do not want to cost a buyer her job by not knowing the rules ahead of time—the last thing you want is to put your
prospect in a compromising situation.

An out-of-office space can be a powerful option, allowing the sales
pro to perform a presentation in a casual, positive, and friendly environment. Be street smart; when appropriate, try a different setting for
your business proposal. You may find more success!

Consider This

Street smart sales pros use well-planned presentations in order to turn
shoppers into buyers. It helps them to discover their prospects' wants
and needs. In addition, it helps them anticipate many of the objections
that they might have to handle. By being well-prepared, street smart
sales pros know where they are going on their sales calls; they do not
like to leave anything to chance. Be street smart—develop a well-
planned presentation; it will keep you from getting lost!

The following eight questions are designed to help you develop a
sales presentation that will work for you. Read these questions, consider them carefully, and answer them on a sheet of paper.

1. Do you have a well-planned presentation?

2. If not, why not?

3. What are the strengths and weaknesses of your product?

4. What gains have your products or services made over the years?

5. Do you know who your competition is?

6. How do your products or services stack up to your competition's?

7. What are some of the unique strengths of your product or service that you can allude to during your presentation?

8. What are some of the features of your product or service that you can use to satisfy customer needs?

You are now in a position to develop and implement a well-planned presentation. If at this point you still believe that sales is best done by an off-the-cuff, ad-libbing kind of approach, then I am afraid that you will not encounter the type of success that you are hoping for. If, on the other hand, you understand that sales involve more than being a fast talker, then you have taken another giant step towards becoming a street smart sales pro.

9

Subliminal Selling

There is a point during street smart sales pros' presentations when their prospects seem to have developed such a level of instant trust and rapport with these adept sales pros that it appears as if a sale will be made with very little additional coaxing. This is due to the fact that street smart sales pros have employed subliminal selling skills, enabling them to influence their prospects subconsciously.

I know what you are thinking—I'm getting a little too carried away with the abilities of these street smart sales pros, now making them out to be some weird mind-controlling product pushers. That's not the case; street smart sales pros are not witch doctors, using their voodoo skills to make sales. What they are using are psychological, body language, and observational techniques in order to gain a valuable selling edge.

If you want to become a street smart subliminal sales pro, positively influencing your prospects on a level they are not aware of, put your negative views in your back pocket and read this chapter carefully. I will teach you the skills necessary to develop a strong bond between you and your prospect. And remember, prospects buy from sales pros they like and believe in.

Observation

Street smart sales pros are aware that one of their greatest sales tools is their sense of observation. These savvy pros make many a sale because through observation, they have picked up valuable clues that often give them a better understanding as to the interests and wants of their prospects.

Knowing the importance of observation, they are like sponges, soaking up everything around them, looking for that one clue that will give them the insight necessary to positively influence the prospects in their favor. These perceptive sales pros know that a prospect's desk or walls can scream out with information that can be invaluable.

By carefully reading this section, you will discover some of the things that street smart sales pros look for in order to make a connection with their prospects. Once you understand the hidden subtleties behind these clues, it will become easier for you to communicate with your prospects, which is essential if you are going to be a successful salesperson.

■ CLASSIFYING YOUR CUSTOMER TYPE

As individuals, we all have unique thought patterns that are influenced by our own environment and interests. Think how helpful it would be for you as a sales pro to have an understanding of how your prospect thinks. How often do you try to communicate with one of your customers, and just don't connect? Many times you write it off, thinking that you're having a bad day, or that your customer is just being a disagreeable so-and-so. The problem is, if you don't know how to zero in on your prospect's thought processes, you will have to rely on the old hit-or-miss method of connecting, which unfortunately leads to many, many days that you will want to write off.

Be street smart; stop guessing how your prospect thinks. Read and study this information carefully; it will help you to think and communicate as your client does.

A fascinating study conducted by Richard Bandler and John Grinder, psychological researchers, led to the conclusion that individuals' thought processes can be influenced by the way information is presented; that is, they either see, hear, or feel what you are saying. They call this neurolinguistic programming, or NLP. They go on to say that prospects fall into three distinct groups: Prospects are visual (lookers), auditory (hearers), or kinesthetic (feelers), according to the way they respond to information and language. Once a sales pro has the ability to discover the group to which his prospect belongs, he then is able to direct his presentation to the level that would most influence his prospect to purchase.

The Lookers

Visual prospects are individuals who respond positively to images such as brochures, colorful pictures, and creative language. When street smart sales pros sell in front of a visual prospect, they consciously use language that will allow their customers to vividly picture the benefits of the product or service they are being sold. Simply put, it is faster and easier for a visual prospect to understand what you are trying to say if you can get him to see your ideas in his mind.

An underachiever, unaware of these three distinct groups of prospects, has no idea to whom he is selling; and if he is lucky enough to build trust and rapport, it is due to chance more than anything else. An underachiever will have enormous difficulty selling to visual prospects if he is using language that inhibits his customers from creating these visual images. So, what are the key characteristics to look for in order to discover if you are indeed selling to a visual prospect? That's a good question, and one that I knew you were going to ask.

When speaking to a visual prospect, you will observe that his eyes move rapidly. This is due to the fact that he is actively trying to picture in his mind exactly what you are saying. Another clue to determine a visual prospect is his use of language. Visual individuals tend to use words that create picture images such as *view, show, bright, picture,* etc. Some typical visual sentences would be:

- "Can you *show* it to me?"
- "That's a really *bright* concept."
- "I can *see* what you mean."
- "That's awesome, I can really *picture* that in my mind."
- "I have a slightly different *view*."

A street smart sales pro, knowing that he is selling to a visual prospect, will employ the following subliminal selling tactics in order to create strong rapport:

Diana, can't you *see* that magnificent car in your driveway? Believe me, I can just *picture* you cruising down the highway. Your friends are going to go crazy when you *show* them that car.

By the time this street smart sales pro has completed his sales presentation, his prospect, on a subconscious level, will not only be able to vividly picture herself driving the car, much to her satisfaction, but she will also feel a bond towards this creative sales pro, making it much easier for her to make a decision to purchase.

Be street smart—when with a visual prospect, sell what she can see; it will help you create those big bucks!

The Listeners

The second group of prospects described by Bandler and Grinder are auditories. These individuals respond most favorably to the way you deliver your information. It is not so much what you say, but more importantly, how you say it through your pitch or tone. These factors have a lot to do with developing rapport with auditory prospects.

Auditories use language that conveys a feeling of sound, such as:

- "Pete, that *sounds* great to me."

- "I'll *call* you next week to discuss it."

- "Go to your room, don't use that *tone* with me."

- "Believe me, I *hear* what you are trying to say."

An auditory frequently puts his hand on his face, as if that will assist him with his hearing. Auditories are not as verbal as visual prospects, since they are thinking over in their mind decisions that they are contemplating making. Over and over again they will verbalize to themselves the pros and cons of the decision.

Back to our street smart car sales pro. Now that he realizes that his prospect is not visual, but is instead auditory, he makes the necessary changes in his presentation to reflect the differences, flexible enough to still be able to develop a strong bond with his customer.

Andrew, when you start up that engine it will be *music* to your *ears*. At seventy miles an hour that car is as *quiet* as a mouse. When you kick it into fourth gear that motor just begins to *sizzle*.

Be street smart—practice these tactics so you will be comfortable using them with auditory prospects. When selling to these types of individuals, use language that builds rapport between the two of you. If you do, when you ask him to purchase, his response will be music to your ears!

The Feelers

The last category of prospects are kinesthetics. These individuals base their decisions more on how they feel than on what they see or hear. They are more emotional and make decisions more from the heart than from the head. Not surprisingly, kinesthetics' vocabulary consists of words like *touch, grab, hold, feel.*

Some typical kinesthetic statements would be:

- "Leah, I know how you *feel.*"

- "I *felt* the same way myself."

- "Tell me how you *feel* about that."

- "I can *appreciate* that myself."

Kinesthetics are "feely" people. They like to hold your products in their hands if possible. You will see them touching samples, brochures, etc. At times they will also reach out to touch you in order to make a point; they are more animated when they speak than the other two groups.

Again we shall return to our street smart car sales pro, this time using subliminal tactics that relate to kinesthetic individuals.

Sarah, just *feel* that leather, isn't it fantastic? Only when you drive down an open highway can you fully *appreciate* how dynamic this car is. All my clients *feel* like teenagers again, especially with *their hair blowing* in the wind.

Be street smart—get these types of customers to feel what you want them to buy; it will touch your heart in the right spot, by making you big bucks!

Now that you are aware of these subtle differences between individuals, the next time you are on a sales call, use your skills of observation to try to discover which category your prospect falls into. It will allow you to establish strong rapport with your prospects that undoubtedly will lead to increased sales, which is the street smart bottom line!

■ ELEMENTARY DEDUCTION

The old saying, "A picture is worth a thousand words," holds true for our street smart sales pro. When he enters a prospect's office, he quickly scans the walls looking for any kind of visual clue that can help him gain insight into his prospect, making mental notes of what he has seen so they can be used when needed in his presentation.

From experience, a street smart sales pro knows that pictures, plaques, or awards tell a great deal about his prospect. Often a client will have pictures that will indicate if he is a sports or hobby enthusiast. There might be a picture of him jogging, playing golf, fishing, running trains, etc. Many top executives, as a result of the pressures of running a company, find sports and hobbies a wonderful outlet for their frustrations and enjoy talking about them.

Street smart sales pros are aware of this, and read up on many different hobbies and sports, just so they will have some information in their bag of selling skills to enable them to ask a question or simply to small talk, all of which goes a long way in building up rapport. Nothing breaks the ice better than asking a prospect about his favorite activity.

If your prospect enjoys an adventurous activity such as flying, this might be an indication that he is not afraid of taking chances with a new product or service. In addition, individuals who take part in activities that could be somewhat dangerous are usually good decision makers and like you to get right to the point. They don't want to dilly dally or hear a lot of bull.

Photographs can indicate if your prospect is a family man and could reveal if there might be another generation coming into the market, a factor that can be especially helpful to you as a sales pro if you are selling a product or service that offers growth, security, and financial stability. After all, as good parents, we certainly do not want to bring our children into a company that will have problems in the future. Street smart sales pros selling consulting services, pension plans, etc., find this information useful.

A plaque, award, or picture can indicate a favorite charity, service, club, or organization that he might serve in for his community. The street smart sales pro uses this bit of information to build rapport by either discussing the various causes or by playing on his prospect's ego by mentioning how much he respects him for getting involved in such a worthy cause. Done in the right manner, this can be extremely beneficial for you on your sales call.

You may come across a client who has a designer showcase for an office, with absolutely no personal mementos. This could indicate that your prospect has strong feelings about the way things appear. In such a situation, a compliment or question about the interior design of the office can go along way.

There are literally hundreds of things to see. Through experience and practice you will be able to discover clues that could make the difference between making the sale or not. Be street smart, look for the clues; it's elementary, my fellow sales pros!

■ DESK MANAGEMENT

There is an old adage, "If a messy desk is a sign of a messy mind, what does an empty desk indicate?" The answer to that question is dependent upon the person with whom you speak. The problem is that there are many interpretations. Psychologists themselves do not agree on what a cluttered or empty desk means with respect to a person's makeup. I have my own theories, but at this point, you would have guessed that.

The Messy Desk

Upon entering an office that appears to be outwardly well run, noticing an executive with a messy desk in this setting would indicate to me that this individual has a hands-on approach in his management style. In addition, many executives with cluttered desks have strong egos, and are not overly concerned with their personal image. These prospects are usually easier to communicate with, allowing you to be fairly informal in your sales approach.

If, on the other hand, the office gives you the impression that the business is only marginal, or that the office does not seem to be well-run, an executive with a messy desk in this scenario might just be over-burdened. Seeing this, you should set up your presentation by being empathetic and indicating to your prospect that using your product or service will help to relieve some of his pressures. If you have to leave various materials behind, such as proposals or brochures, make sure that there is something visible on your paperwork that will allow it to stand out so it will not be lost in his sea of other paperwork.

The Clean Desk

A clean desk may indicate several character types.These executives very often are image conscious. They may also dress accordingly; in many instances, these individuals like formality.

In some cases, clean desk enthusiasts may be obsessive-compulsive individuals who have fixed routines, want things placed in their right-ful places, and are sticklers for details. They appreciate straightfor-wardness. When you leave the office of such people, always make sure to put your chair back where you found it.

In other cases, some clean desks indicate that an individual wants to be seen as keeping up with his workload, even if it's not quite the case. In one situation, a client confessed to me that he was actually swamped with work, but kept the bulk of his work files out of sight, in his closet. These people are more informal, but nervous. As you size up your prospect, make sure your presentation reflects the individual sitting behind the desk.

Be street smart—pay attention to your prospect's desk; it could help you clean up.

Subliminal Selling

As a result of using certain psychological techniques, street smart sales pros are able to develop a real selling edge. These techniques are so subtle that their prospects for the most part are not aware that they are being influenced by them.

Many of these techniques have been used to influence you to make various day-to-day decisions, either through television, magazine, radio, or newspaper advertising. Did you ever wonder why you buy a certain cereal, drink a certain soda, etc.? Advertisers have been aware of these tactics for years; now you have an opportunity to learn them. Be street smart, read this section very carefully; it's a psychologically sound idea!

■ TRIGGER WORDS

In a study done at Yale, researchers reported that there are certain key words that trigger a positive response in individuals. These findings were published by the National Association of Insurance and Financial Advisors. The study disclosed what they felt were the twelve most influential words to your customers' ears. By using these words, you will better be able to establish rapport and trust with your prospect. Street smart sales pros use these trigger words as much as possible in their day-to-day selling, via the telephone, their sales calls, or in their correspondence materials.

The following list of twelve words will prove to be invaluable to you. These are the words that the researchers found provoked positive responses in individuals. Read, study, and use them on your sales calls. They will help you to influence your prospect on a subliminal level in your favor.

1. *Discover.* People like to be part of a new discovery. When the people behind a new credit card company needed a name that would be able to compete against the three giants of the industry, Master Card, Visa, and American Express, they came up with the "Discover Card." It was based on extensive research.

2. *Easy.* Prospects like to be able to purchase with ease; they are tired of the day-to-day complexities of life.

3. *Guarantee.* People are afraid to be cheated; they react positively to products or services that offer guarantees.

4. *Health.* Health is the most important thing to individuals, and that includes money. As a prospect gets older, health becomes more precious.

5. *Love.* Everybody reacts uniquely to the word; it is the most emotional word in our vocabulary.

6. *Money.* Everybody wants it, and I mean everybody. Even the rich can't get enough of it.

7. *New.* If it's new, we assume it just has to be better.

8. *Proven.* Proven gives the impression that something is tried and true; it just plain works. People want things they can depend on.

9. *Results.* Results convey a positive bottom line image. "This product gives results." People like that; it makes them feel that they will be getting what they paid for.

10. *Safety.* Products that are safe conjure up trust and reliability, features that prospects want.

11. *Save.* Everybody enjoys a savings, either in dollars or time.

12. *You.* Using the word *you* personalizes your approach, making your prospect feel as if he were special. People like to feel special.

Practice using these words. If *you* do, *you* will *discover* how *easy* it is to influence your prospects, *saving* you precious time trying to convince them that your products are indeed *safe, healthy,* and *proven* to produce the *results* promised. If *you* do, I *guarantee* that you will *love* how well your prospects will respond.

Be street smart; use these techniques—they will lead to big money.

■ SUBLIMINAL COMMANDS

The street smart sales pro uses subliminal commands to assure his prospects that they are doing the right thing by deciding to purchase. The technique is simple; in order to get his prospects to remember important aspects of his presentation, the street smart sales pro will emphasize certain words or phrases in a statement that will reinforce as well as draw attention back to a point or benefit of his product or service.

- "Jerry, *you will benefit* from this program just the way all my other clients who have *purchased* have benefited."

- "When you *own* this car it will make you feel young again."

- "I know this product *will work for you.*"

- "Based on what you've said, I know you will *gain enormous satisfaction.*"

A subliminal command can also be effective if you use a phrase that a prospect seems to favor. If a prospect frequently says, "This is the greatest thing since sliced bread," to indicate that something is special, you can take this statement and use it as a subliminal command.

- "Bill, this program is the *greatest thing since sliced bread;* you are going to enjoy it."

Be street smart, practice using this subliminal technique; I know you will be successful.

■ TACTICAL IMPLIED SELLING

The street smart sales pro, by phrasing a statement in a certain way, can subliminally influence his prospects to assume that his products or services have unique strengths. These artful sales pros are then able to create an image in their prospects' minds, convincing them that they are dealing with a company that has special qualities. Individuals like to do business with companies that have special qualities. The following statement, made by a street smart home improvement sales pro, will illustrate this point:

> The people who will be installing your windows, Mr. Brown, *work only for us. We do not subcontract our work.* This enables us to control the quality of installation, insuring that you will have no problems in the future.

By making a statement such as the one above, the street smart sales pro is allowing his client to assume that employing one's own installation employees is unique to the industry. This may or may not be the case. What is important is that the client perceives it as a benefit.

Consider all the areas of strength that you might be able to use to your advantage when speaking to a potential customer. Areas of possible unique strengths that you can look to include in your presentation are:

- Client Base
- People
- Delivery
- Product
- Experience
- Reputation
- Inventory
- Service

Include these unique strengths to your advantage in your presentation; it's the street smart thing to do!

■ COLOR POWER

The street smart sales pro is aware of how color can affect his prospects and, as a result, he uses it on a subliminal level in order to influence his customers in his favor.

If you doubt the power of color, which car do you perceive to go faster, a red Porsche or a brown Porsche? The majority of people absolutely believe the red one. Advertisers have long understood the power of color. When you are looking through a magazine, see how often red is used when trying to convey speed. On the other hand, if an advertiser is trying to get across an image of invincibility, you will see the color brown displayed prominently. A brown eighteen-wheeler is a heck of a lot sturdier than a pink one, isn't it?

Knowing this, the street smart sales pro incorporates color into his presentation on a subliminal level in order to gain trust and rapport between himself and his prospect. After reading this, you may decide that it is time to throw out a few of your business clothes, finally realizing that they just weren't the right fit!

Studies have indicated that there are three colors that clearly have a positive subliminal effect on an individual. The colors navy blue, dove gray, and charcoal gray will create an image of leadership, stability, security, and success. These colors should make it into your presentation, incorporated into either your dress or your support materials:

- *Navy Blue.* People associate stability and leadership with the color blue, which is the reason why so many politicians choose to wear navy suits. The next time you are watching a debate on television, just look at how many of the candidates look as if they purchased their clothes off the same rack! Companies that spend money on brochures would be wise to incorporate blue throughout, especially in their logo. Visual prospects respond well to sales pros who wear blue suits.

- *Dove Gray.* Dove gray creates an image of stability and security in an individual's mind. If you are not sure that this is true, think about the color of security trucks, as well as the fact that most airport terminals are painted dove gray. A tie of dove gray is a nice subliminal touch with a blue suit.

- *Charcoal Gray.* Charcoal gray is a slightly more formal alternative to dove gray. Because it is a darker color, charcoal connotes seriousness and strength of purpose, but avoids the funereal effect that a black suit can project. Moreover, charcoal gray flatters many different complexions and matches well with a variety of colors.

The studies also have found that the three worst colors are black, which people associate with death; purple, associated with sickness; and yellow, associated with high anxiety. In fact, they discovered that the color yellow actually was able to increase anxiety and blood pressure levels in a short period of time. In addition, people over fifty found yellow to be the most irritating color to the retina.

Common sense also dictates that you avoid using any bright or loud colors. Red in particular can be perceived as a "power" color—an accent can be used effectively, but too much, and you risk intimidating or threatening your prospect.

Now that you know the power of color, use it to your advantage with your prospects. You will find it especially effective with your visual clients.

Be street smart—let navy blue, dove gray, and charcoal gray find their way into your clothes and support materials; it will lead to big green bucks!

Body Language

Street smart sales pros have known for a long time that a great deal of communication can go on without anyone uttering a sound. Body language often says a great deal more than the spoken word. A raised eyebrow, a slouch of the shoulders, and a nod of a head are examples of how individuals can send meaningful signals to each other, and in many instances people are not aware that they are sending them.

In this section, you will learn how to interpret your prospect's body language, as well as how you can use your own body language to advantage on sales calls. Be street smart—read this section carefully; understand how the unspoken word can be mightier than the sword!

■ HANDSHAKES

For most of us, a handshake is simply a greeting between two people, but not for our street smart sales pro. A handshake offers valuable clues, clues that just might tell him a little bit more about his prospect and help in successfully completing a sale. The following handshakes will describe to you just how much you can actually learn about an individual without having him utter a single word:

- *Firm Handshake.* A firm handshake indicates that your prospect is a tough, bottom-line person. He will not be easily intimidated, and you'd better have the facts to back up your statements.

- *Upper Handshake.* In this unique style of handshake, an individual places his hand in a horizontal position on top of yours, squeezing it in a vise-like fashion, thus giving a strong indication that you will not be talking to anyone closely resembling Mr. Rogers or anybody in his neighborhood. These individuals can be tough and abrasive, and have a definite need to always remain in control. Can you say the word "intimidating?" As a sales pro, you cannot allow yourself to be intimidated. You don't want to lose control of your sales call, for if you do, your chances of successfully completing a sale are slim.

If during your sales call a prospect is rude or abrasive, it is best for you to stop your presentation and address the problem by saying:

Luke, I don't understand why you seem to be so annoyed with my being here. If I said anything to offend you I apologize; believe me, I am here to help you, I am on your side. Are you just having a bad day?

or

Matt, I came here with the best of intentions, yet I feel hostility on your part towards me. What seems to be bothering you?

Wait for his response; it may surprise you. By making this kind of direct statement, confronting someone's poor manners, you will most likely catch him off guard and he often will either apologize or discuss what is concerning him, which may have absolutely nothing to do with you. This approach will help you regain control of the sales call, frequently putting your prospect on the defensive. Most individuals do not intend to be rude. More importantly, this will help you keep your own self-respect; nobody should allow himself to be abused.

- *Dead Fish Handshake.* This kind of handshake may indicate that your prospect is nervous or unsure of himself. Keeping that in mind, the street smart sales pro uses a lot of empathy on this sales call, constantly reassuring his prospect that he is making a wise decision to purchase. Individuals displaying this type of personality might need some added pressure in order to make a decision.

- *No Handshake at All.* Not a great sign. This prospect probably regrets the day that he agreed to see you. Knowing this, the street smart sales pro tries to pick up any additional clues in order to try to break the ice by talking about something that is close to his client's heart, such as television, his family, or his favorite charity.

■ EYE TALKING

The street smart sales pro is aware that a lot can be learned through his prospect's eyes. Consider the customer who blinks in rhythmic beats or deliberately looks away from you; he is sending you the message that he was not really receptive to what you just said in your sales presentation. At that point it is essential for you to clarify your point with him in order to try to get agreement.

Go over the information, then look sincerely into his eyes and ask, "Mark, you look as if you have some concerns over what I just said; what are they?" Listen for her response. After you have clarified your point, he may indicate that he has no concerns, or he may tell you that he feels what you have said holds no water; and if that's the case, at least you now know what objection you will have to overcome in order to make the sale.

Prospects who are in deep thought, considering what you are saying, generally have their eyes focused on a stationary object. They do this, as opposed to looking at you, because they do not want to be interrupted. Let your prospect think, even if you have to pull out some paper work, pretending to do some figuring. When he wants to resume the sales call, he will turn his head back to you, which is a signal to move on. You might ask, "Randy, you look like you were in deep thought; is there anything you want to share or question?" Often he will let you in on what he was thinking, which can help you enormously in completing a successful sales call.

When a prospect continually looks away from you while he is talking, and all the while his eyes are moving from side to side as if he were watching a ping-pong game, there is an excellent chance that this prospect is lying to you. The only thing that you can do is to make one of the following statements:

- "Paul, are you absolutely sure about your facts?"

- "Gee, Chris, I've been in the business a long time and I've never heard that one; are you sure?"

- "You're going away for a week; let's set another appointment for a day after you come back."

Frequently a prospect will know that you have caught him in a lie, and, by making a statement like the above, you give him an opportunity to get out of his lie.

The street smart sales pro can use his eyes to convey many, many moods, such as empathy, enthusiasm, sorrow, and confidence. When shaking hands with prospects, he looks straight into their eyes with a nice big smile that indicates confidence in himself. When the sales call is over, even if it was not successful, he does the same thing, never leaving with his head or eyes down, which would convey the feeling of defeat.

If a street smart sales pro wants to give his prospect his best power stare, indicating that he is one tough confident cookie, he slightly closes his eyes, slowly moving them from side to side, concentrating not to blink. This kind of look can be very intimidating to the person you are staring at.

Using your eyes to convey different moods takes practice. By using a mirror you can practice using your eyes to express different frames of mind, such as joy, anger, sorrow, etc. After a while, practice with friends by having them guess the feeling you are trying to express.

Be street smart—listen to what your prospect's eyes are telling you; it could help you see those large commission checks!

■ GESTURES

Prospects make statements through slight movements of their bodies, which can give you valuable insight as to how or what they are thinking. For this reason, street smart sales pros look intently for that frown, shrug, or what-have-you in order to pick up a clue that can help them to complete a sale successfully. Underachievers rarely pick up any of this information, severely limiting their ability to achieve. If, during your sales presentation, you observe your prospect nodding his head in agreement with what you are saying, it might be in your best interest to ask for the order.

On the other hand, a prospect who has a frown on his forehead, all the while rubbing his chin, is sending you a message that he has some concerns that must be addressed promptly or there will be no chance for a sale. At this point, look deeply into your prospect's eyes, opening your eyes wide to give you a Bambi-like appearance that conveys sincerity, and ask, "Ian, I get the feeling that there is something bothering you, what is it?" Many times, as a result of your eyes expressing sincere concern, the prospect will tell you exactly what is on his mind, which should help you enormously in successfully completing that sales call.

Prospects show disinterest or boredom either by pretending to pick off particles from their clothing or by rubbing their eyes and foreheads. The message is clear: They can't wait for you to leave their office. If you see that your prospect is about to go into a coma, change your tone of voice, become more animated with your hands, and immediately direct some questions to him that just might stir up some interest on his part.

Alex, I'm doing all the talking, let me ask you a question. What would you like to see happen if you engaged a company like my own?

Wait for his response, get him to talk; even if he expresses that he doesn't have much interest, at least he is getting involved. Once you know his feelings and concerns, you have a starting point to work on.

A prospect who subtly uses his fingers to either rub the side of his nose or cover his lips, occasionally forcing a cough that is as phony as Paul Shaffer's fake laugh on *The Late Show with David Letterman*, is telling you that he is skeptical. If you see this occurring, pause briefly, conveying the feeling of thought on your part, and ask:

> Karl, I get extremely excited talking about my product/service and at times my prospects interpret my enthusiasm as an exaggeration on my part about how they will benefit from my product/service. Do you think that I have been exaggerating?

The fantastic thing about this approach is that your prospect will tell you if he believes you have exaggerated, which gives you an opportunity to deal with this objection and, if done successfully, to make a sale.

Street smart sales pros use body language in order to send messages to their customers. If used properly, body language can indicate that they are confident and enthusiastic about what they are doing. These apt sales pros know that if they sit in front of a prospect with little movement, stiff as a board, it will send the message to their prospects that they are nervous and unsure of themselves.

When a street smart sales pro wishes to make an emphatic point, he will put his fingers together while raising his hand in the air. Moving it in this manner gives the impression that he is chopping wood. Former President Bill Clinton used this technique very effectively. If your prospect is not following your chopping motion with his eyes, it indicates that his mind is someplace else—and if you are going to make the sale, you had better bring it back.

An individual who talks with a limp wrist conveys the feeling to his prospect that he is weak. A stiff wrist, clenched fist, and strong upper arm movement will cure you of this problem.

Be street smart—understand and use body language to your advantage!

■ MIRRORING

An excellent subliminal tactic employed by the street smart sales pro is a technique called mirroring. Studies have found that it is possible to develop high rapport with clients through nonverbal mimicking of their body actions. If a prospect crosses his legs, you cross your legs; if a prospect puts his hands to his face, you put your hands to your face. The street smart sales pro does this in such a subtle manner that his prospect is not aware that he is being mimicked. Nevertheless, this tactic helps to establish fantastic rapport, making it much easier for these savvy sales pros to successfully complete their sales.

How many times have you been on a sales call when your prospect has been ill at ease, rude, or simply not that interested in what you had to say? By using this tactic, you can develop rapport that will relax your prospect as well as gain his interest in what you are saying. This physical empathy is essential to your success, and will amaze you with how effective it is at disarming even the toughest of clients.

Be street smart; don't be too heavy-handed about mirroring. Do it subtly and see how you can improve your rapport with clients, making your sales calls go much more smoothly!

■ BODY POSITIONING

In addition to the gestures you and your prospect make, you must also be aware of the way your body is positioned relative to that of your prospect. Nearly everyone is familiar with the *Seinfeld* episode in which Elaine brings over her new boyfriend, Aaron, who is a "close talker"— a guy who stands unpleasantly close to others when he is talking with them. Don't be a close talker! Respect other people's personal space.

The street smart sales pro knows that the placement of his body can be construed as a power play. Too close, and his prospect will be intimidated or threatened; too distant, and the prospect will think the sales rep is disinterested or, worse, put off. The street smart sales pro positions himself in a way that will put the prospect at ease; he works hard to put himself on the same level as the client, establishing a certain physical equality. If the prospect stands, so does the sales pro; if the prospect sits, so, too, does the sales pro (assuming he has the prospect's permission). Always directly face your client; this is a stance that demonstrates openness and a readiness to listen. You can lean in ever so slightly towards your prospect in order to show interest, but don't go too far. A sales pro will never tower over his customer, invade his personal space, or unexpectedly touch the prospect; all these moves frighten off the client and make him less likely to buy.

Years ago, there was never a second thought when a sales rep touched a customer's shoulder or arm, or even patted a back. In fact, these physical gestures were often deliberately used in order to promote familiarity and a feeling of closeness! Today, however, the rules of contact have greatly changed. Unless you have a very close relationship with the individual you are dealing with, you should refrain from any body contact beyond a handshake.

Be street smart; watch your body positioning! Make your prospect comfortable, and he'll soon want to buy!

■ DEVELOPING YOUR SUBLIMINAL TECHNIQUES

Observational, psychological, and physical techniques are not exact sciences that can guarantee you perfect results. What they give you is an edge, an opportunity to send and gather information that can be helpful to you during a sales call. These skills, like any other skills, have to be developed; until they are, you will not be able to pick up all the valuable information that is available to you.

The more you try to incorporate subliminal tactics such as trigger words into your sales presentation, the better and more comfortable you will be in utilizing these techniques. The same holds true with respect to body language. To master these techniques, you have to practice the basic skills. Start off slowly, using the mirroring technique. Concentrate on your prospect's eyes, gestures, etc. You will be surprised how much this ability will help you on your sales calls.

Your observational skills also have to be developed. After all, it would be impossible for me to give you all the variables that could come about through observation. Only through experience and practice will you be able to pick up and use these clues to your advantage. The following exercise will help you to develop a keen sense of observation.

Pick a room in your house and walk into it for ten seconds. Then go in another room and write down everything that you observed, trying to be as specific as possible. Then return to the room and see what you left out. Go to different rooms of your house each day and use this exercise. When you are finished going through each room of your house, start observing your closets, by opening them for about five seconds.

While at work, observe how your fellow workers walk, talk, dress, shake hands, manage their desks, etc. Go into friends' offices and quickly look around, writing down all the things that you saw. Go back and see what you might have missed. In a short period of time, this exercise will help you develop a keen sense of observation, wherein it will become second nature for you to pick up on most of your prospect's subtle, but important, nuances.

Consider This

Be street smart—become the sponge and clean up, by making those big sales!

The following ten questions are designed to get you to begin to use these subliminal tactics during your day-to-day sales calls. Read these questions, consider them carefully, and answer them on a sheet of paper.

1. Presently, do you use observation to help you during your sales calls?

2. Specifically, what changes would you have to make in your current presentation in order to use the subliminal tactics on visual, auditory, and kinesthetic individuals?

3. Generally, what colors are your business clothes?

4. Would you find it difficult to use the mirroring tactic?

5. If so, why?

6. Specifically, what tactics would you use in order to incorporate the twelve trigger words into your presentation?

7. When you walk into a prospect's office, what are some of the things that you look for?

8. What do you look for in your prospect's body language that could help you during your sales call?

9. Presently, are you using body language as a sales tactic?

10. If not, why not?

I know even at this point that there are still a few doubters who do not believe in the effectiveness of subliminal selling. That's fine, as long as you are willing to give it a try. If you are not, you will be allowing yourself to lose out on a valuable selling skill.

The individuals who believe now have the information necessary to influence prospects on a level that they are not aware of. Practice these tactics; once you have gained the experience to plant positive seeds in your customer's head, you then have taken a major step towards becoming a street smart sales pro.

10

Tactics for Overcoming Fear

In Chapter 4, "Like What You See," I stated that a key element necessary for the street smart sales pro to achieve greatness is to have a positive self-image. I pointed out how there are two variables, one internal and the other external, that influence the development of a person's self-esteem.

The internal factors are directly related to the way an individual perceives herself, as well as the way she believes others see her. The external factors have to do with the individual's surrounding environment, including her job. Depending on the way an individual sees herself, internal and external factors can either be translated into positive or negative behavior.

Street smart sales pros translate these internal and external factors into positive behavior. They will not allow their fears, anxieties, or poor self-images to get the better of them. They realize that if they allowed this to happen, they would not be able to function at their highest levels, and they refuse to accept this!

Read this chapter carefully. Learn to develop the techniques that will teach you how to confront your problems, deal with them, and overcome them; it's the street smart thing to do.

■ TAUGHT TO FEAR

The majority of factors that cause us fear, anxiety, and low self-esteem are taught to us by others. These lessons are well learned and keep many of us from performing at our highest levels. We are conditioned not to try to achieve greatness. A parent who, with all the best intentions, tells her child to take a particular job because it will be easy, safe, and secure, is really telling her child that he does not have what it takes to achieve greatness. We are conditioned to stay away from certain courses, professions, and accounts, because others have told us that they are too difficult, that we would not be able to succeed. Unfortunately, many of us are listening to underachievers, to individuals who were too scared to take the action in their own lives that was necessary to achieve greatness.

Why do you think so many children are scared to death of dogs? Certainly, we are not born with the fear of dogs, nor for that matter of any other animals. It's because parents have done an excellent job of warning their children that if they get too close to one of these mongrels, they just might get one of their hands bitten off.

I had a dog who was so old that he could hardly see or hear. On top of this, he was in dire need of dentures. Nevertheless, every time my grown cousin came over to my house and my dog just happened to wander into his path, he would go totally berserk, as if he were about to be eaten alive. My aunt did one helluva job of instilling the fear of dogs in my cousin.

When a parent screams at a toddler to stay away from a hot stove, the intent of the parent is to keep that child from being burnt. Warned a number of times, the toddler develops a fear of that stove and learns to stay away from it. In some instances, however, upon hearing a parent yell, the toddler begins to cry, not really knowing what to be afraid of. The fear the toddler feels can transfer to other related objects, people, or situations.

When we are children, our peers can negatively influence how we feel about ourselves. Everybody wants to be socially accepted and liked. When we become the butt of others' cruel jokes or comments, we tend to withdraw, and we develop poor self-images. The many individuals who base their self-esteem on others soon end up miserable, frustrated, and depressed.

As we get older, we see how we might become afraid under certain circumstances, especially by subconsciously accepting others' fears as our own. A statement such as, "I'm scared to death of speaking in front of people," is an example of how a negative thought of others can influence the way we think and react. That is one of the reasons why so many individuals have problems speaking in front of groups.

From early on we are conditioned to fear change. That is why so many people use the word "no" as if it were an involuntary response to being asked to make a decision. Think about it; when you go into a clothing store and a salesperson comes up to you and says, "Can I help you?" what is your first response? "No, I'm just looking." "No" insures that the status quo will remain. Individuals who are afraid of change limit their chances to achieve greatness because of their lack of confidence in themselves. They are prisoners of their own self-destructive insecurities.

In many instances, individual fears can appear to make little sense. On one hand, a person can be terrified to speak in front of a class, yet amazingly enough have no fear of sky diving. Nevertheless, no matter how nonsensical fears might be, they are still real to the individuals who experience them. Fears can lead to feelings of inferiority, shyness, and extreme anxiety.

Individuals who have inferiority complexes are basically fearful people who see themselves as less worthy, constantly putting themselves down by verbalizing their own self-defeat, rejection, and low self-esteem. When you feel inferior, having low self-esteem, you truly are afraid to face life with all its highs and lows. People who feel inferior use phrases such as, "I could never do that," "That's beyond me," or "I'm just an ordinary Joe."

Fears can be so terrible that you can develop anxiety and apprehensions about things that may or may not happen. People can't sleep at night because they have anxiety about the possibility of being audited. Sales pros start to sweat profusely because they fear that a prospect may have a complaint or a question that they might not know how to answer.

Street smart sales pros understand that if fears, anxieties, and poor self-esteem are learned, they can also be unlearned. Read, study, and learn to unlearn everything that's keeping you from achieving at the highest level.

■ IDENTIFYING YOUR FEARS AND ANXIETIES

Street smart sales pros are willing to confront their fears and anxieties head on. They are aware that this is the only way that they will be able to overcome them. It may involve forcing themselves to solicit on the telephone, or confronting their bosses regarding a particular concern.

Street smart sales pros are keenly aware that if they did not confront their problems, and instead played it close to the chest, they would miss out on enormous opportunities and happiness in life. The individual who is terrified to ask a guy for a date misses out on all the pleasures associated with dating. The sales pro who is afraid to solicit the large accounts will never have the opportunity of achieving those large commission checks.

Before you can confront and overcome a fear or anxiety, you have to be able to identify it. That is the only way you can truly understand what you are up against. The street smart tactic that you will use is to make a list of all your fears and anxieties. For this to be effective, you have to include as much detail as possible, including people, situations, or thoughts that are causing you to have anxiety. It is important for you to describe how these fears and anxieties are affecting you emotionally and mentally. Lastly, include a history of your fears and anxieties, starting with your earliest recollections and ending with your last experience. Below is an example of how this should look on your piece of paper:

My Fears

1. *Talking to a group.* Whenever I have to make a presentation, I become irritable and unable to sleep, and I develop stomach cramps. The first time I can remember feeling this way was when I had to make a speech about Abraham Lincoln in front of my fifth grade class. Last week I had to make a presentation to a group of buyers, and the same old feeling came out.

2. *Making a decision.* I become nervous and clammy every time I have to make a decision. The first time I can remember feeling lousy about making a decision was when I was trading some baseball cards with some friends and I heard someone say that I was a jerk. Last month I walked out of a car showroom because I became so uncomfortable about making a decision regarding which color I should choose.

Now that you have identified what your fears or anxieties are, you will be able to concentrate on overcoming them. Read the next section carefully; it will provide you with the street smart tactics necessary to deal with your problems and concerns.

■ THE TACTIC OF VISUALIZATION

Once a street smart sales pro identifies her problems, one of the techniques that she uses to overcome them is called visualization. Visualization is a process whereby the street smart sales pro pictures in her mind an upcoming event that normally would cause her to have fear or anxiety. Instead of allowing this image in her mind to cause her discomfort, the street smart sales pro learns to visualize herself responding in a confident, positive manner, which helps to eliminate her fear and anxiety.

Daydreaming is a form of visualization. When your daydreams are positive, they help you relax. The positive commands that your daydreams send to your brain keep you happy and alert, which enables you to achieve at a higher level than you normally can.

The day before a big game, professional athletes often dream about the game, vividly picturing themselves performing a particular feat. They find that this helps them to mentally prepare themselves. And just like the professional athlete, you are going to create positive visualizations that will mentally prepare you to overcome your fears or anxieties.

Let's suppose one of the events that cause you a great deal of anxiety surfaces when you have to make a presentation in front of a large account. Close your eyes and start picturing this scenario in your mind. You are greeted with a warm smile by your prospect, who gives you every reason to believe that she is happy to see you. As you are going through your presentation, you are handling all of her questions and objections in a logical, convincing manner, much to the satisfaction of your customer. Finally, picture yourself shaking your prospect's hand, walking out with the signed contract.

In order for visualization to work, you have to follow some simple rules. Most importantly, your visualization always has to be positive. It will only create more discomfort if you allow negative images to enter your mind. If you visualize a prospect who is rude and obnoxious, you will experience even more anxiety before that sales call.

Also, the more detailed your visualizations are, the more effective they will become. See yourself writing up your sales contract. Picture that smile on your prospect's face. Imagine how happy you are putting that signed contract in your attaché case. Look carefully; you're smiling.

Finally, practice this technique. The more you use it, the more effective visualization will be for you. Give this technique a chance; it works. You will see that any situation that causes you to have fear or anxiety can be overcome through visualization by creating a positive solution of that event.

Be street smart—picture yourself as a winner; it will help you overcome many obstacles.

■ THE TACTIC OF AFFIRMATION

Many people are their own worst enemies, unwittingly putting themselves down. They plainly don't like themselves. Street smart sales pros avoid doing this by using the technique of affirmation. Affirmative statements are positive commands that you give to yourself in order to keep your motivation level high. While to some, this may sound a bit off-the-wall, studies have repeatedly shown that reprogramming the mind can alter the way we see ourselves.

This specific technique is essential, for unless you make a real effort to think positively, negative thoughts will eventually creep into your mind, causing you to become hesitant, unsure, depressed, and frustrated, all the while feeling poorly about yourself.

For individuals who suffer from anxiety, the following affirmations should be used frequently:

- "I am a good person, I deserve success."

- "I am good. In fact, it's frightening how good I am."

- "Nothing is going to stop me from succeeding; I have the ability to achieve greatness."

An excellent technique for people who don't feel positive is to wake up in the morning and say, "It's great to be alive." When you first look into that mirror, you must see yourself as a winner, able to achieve greatness. "I like you, you're going to do great things today. Nobody, and I mean nobody, is going to stop you from becoming a champion."

At the end of each day, write down all the positive things that took place. Even if there was a setback, write down what you learned from the experience, turning a negative situation into a positive one. If, for example, you do not make a sale the first time, you then would say, "I learned a lot from this sales call, I'll get him the next time," and when you do, you'll say, "I am good!"

When they close a sale, street smart sales pros unconsciously say to themselves, "I am good." They are not blowing their own horns or trying to put someone else down by telling themselves how good they are; what they are doing is confirming their belief in themselves through positive affirmations.

In order to get the most out of this technique, follow these rules:

- Make your affirmations as specific as possible. If you have problems giving group presentations, simply say, "I have everything under control. I know my demonstration is going to go very well."

- Affirmations should always be positively worded commands. If you say, "I am not scared of this presentation," the use of the word *scared* conveys a negative feeling. Instead you should phrase your affirmation in this manner: "I am confident and prepared to make an excellent presentation."

- Reinforce your affirmations with positive visualizations. If you see yourself acting with confidence, back this image up with affirmative commands.

Street smart sales pros would be the first to tell you that everybody has setbacks. But by seeing yourself as a winner, continually talking in positive terms to yourself, you will be able to keep your spirits and motivation high enough to achieve great success. Be street smart, talk positively to yourself; it will make you perform better.

■ OVERCOMING THE FEAR OF TALKING

A common fear among individuals is the fear of talking in front of a group. Even though sales pros earn their living by talking, often they are not comfortable speaking either to a large account or in a group situation, especially when they have to make demonstrations. Because speaking to an important account or group is so essential to your success, I am treating this particular fear as a separate topic, giving you additional insight as to how to overcome it.

As previously discussed, you can use the tactics of visualization and affirmation to help overcome this particular fear. By visualizing yourself making a strong, confident presentation and combining it with affirmative statements such as, "I know I sound confident," you will go a long way towards solving this problem.

In addition to visualization and affirmation techniques, whether you know it or not, there are a host of other things that you can do to overcome this fear. There are courses in public speaking that are offered at your local community centers, high schools, or colleges. There are courses given by private self-help companies such as Dale Carnegie, which will provide you with helpful hints in public speaking. The Phobia Society of America is a nationwide group of therapists, doctors, and recovering phobics who give all sorts of valuable information as to how to deal with your problem. There are also many worthwhile books that you can read that can help you deal with this fear. You'll find the names of the authors and their titles in the resource section in the back of the book. And just remember, that you are not alone. There are a number of celebrities who have had similar fears of speaking in front of the public, including Bruce Willis, Julia Roberts, Harrison Ford, and Tiger Woods to mention just a few.

As you should do with any kind of activity that you are uncomfortable with, sit down and critique your performance after practicing it, noting the changes that will improve it. Then go through the process over again, asking your friends or relatives to see if there was any improvement. Go through this process over and over again until you feel that you have conquered the fear of communicating; it's the street smart thing to do!

■ REWARDS AND PUNISHMENTS TACTICS

Whenever a street smart sales pro forces herself to make a significant effort to overcome something that causes her anxiety, she rewards herself with something special. It could be clothes, a night out, some type of treat. The important thing is that she knows that she deserves this special prize for trying, no matter if she is successful or not.

On the other hand, if she procrastinates and just doesn't put in the effort to try to perform, she gives herself a punishment. It might be cleaning out her closets, washing her car, or sitting in on a weekend.

Be street smart—do what you have to, then reward yourself for a job well tried.

■ RELAXATION TACTICS

It is extremely important for you to learn how to relax. Individuals who are always tense have a difficult time identifying as well as solving any of their problems.

It is not unusual for people who are nervous, tense, or feeling highly anxious to start breathing rapidly, which causes them to get dizzy, which causes them to become even more upset and scared. The dizziness comes from the increased oxygen that enters the blood stream as a result of rapid breathing. Obviously, it becomes virtually impossible for individuals to solve any of their problems under these conditions. And, of course, merely being told to relax usually doesn't do the trick. However, when a street smart sales pro experiences these feelings, she goes through one of her relaxation techniques in order to get herself to calm down.

If you feel sudden anxiety before a sales presentation, try this exercise. Close your eyes and take a deep breath, all the while tightening every muscle in your body. Stay in this position for approximately six to eight seconds, then let your breath out. At that point, with your eyes still closed, breathe in a rhythmic pattern for twenty seconds. Repeat this routine three times; by the end, you should feel more relaxed, allowing you to deal with your anxiety.

When you are feeling fatigued and tense at the end of the day, try this method to relax. For twenty minutes or so, with your eyes closed, focus all your attention on one word or a fixed point in your mind. The greater your ability to focus your mind on the word or point the more relaxed you will become.

Lastly, listening to soft, soothing music can be very relaxing. The street smart sales pro always has a few of these CDs or radio stations in her car in order to clear her head before her next appointment.

Be street smart, practice these techniques; a sales pro who is tense will invariably make her prospect tense. And customers who are tense do not buy!

■ ARE YOU TALKING TO ME?

Street smart sales pros work very hard at keeping up a positive, upbeat attitude. They are aware that if they are going to achieve greatness, it is essential that they remain motivated. They use the techniques of visualization (seeing themselves as winners) and affirmation (telling themselves they are winners) in order to keep themselves positive. In addition to these techniques, they know the importance of associating themselves with individuals who are winners and have a good attitude about life.

It can be extremely stimulating and motivating when you are in the company of people with high aspirations. If you need a push or a boost, invariably you will be able to get it from these types of individuals. By being with positive people, you tend to reinforce your positive thinking.

As we learned in Chapter 4, negative people can help destroy an individual's self-image and motivation. Because of this, street smart sales pros stay away from these types of individuals as if they have the plague, and in a way they do, for they are carriers of self-destruction. The tactic a street smart sales pro uses if she happens to find herself trapped in the company of a negative person is simply to tell her to stop being so negative.

At times, individuals are so down and depressed that they are not aware that they are being so negative, and they occasionally will thank you for your honesty. If you notice that the people you are hanging around are still negative and won't change their attitude, remember, you have the option to make new friends.

The next time you hear someone trying to contaminate your thinking, be street smart and leave, and I mean leave!

■ USE WHAT'S OUT THERE

Self-help materials are used by the street smart sales pro to reinforce all his positive thoughts. There are self-help books just like the one you are reading right this second that can give you invaluable insight and information. There are also self-help CDs, DVDs, and podcasts that you can watch or listen to at home. For examples, see our *Resources* section on page 193.

There are a variety of public speaking courses available. Some are offered through local community centers and high schools. By making a few phone calls or doing a quick Internet search, you can learn where these local courses are given. Private and national organizations, such as the Dale Carnegie Institute, also offer courses; consult the *Resources* section on page 193 for more information. I don't particularly like using online courses—just how good can a course on public speaking be if you don't actually have to face other people in order to complete it?

Be street smart, investigate all the self-help avenues that are out there for you; they just might offer you the support needed to achieve the greatness you are after.

Consider This

Street smart sales pros use these tactics for overcoming fear to gain control over their lives. They are aware that it would be impossible for them to perform at their highest level if their minds were constantly preoccupied with doom and gloom. Be street smart; practice these tactics and remember what President Franklin D. Roosevelt said, "The only thing we have to fear is fear itself."

The following nine guidelines are designed for you to better understand and practice these techniques. Relax long enough to read these concerns, think about them carefully, and answer them on a sheet of paper.

1. Make a list describing all your fears and anxieties.

2. Go through each of the above and use the techniques of visualization and affirmation in order to help you deal with these concerns.

3. Do you like yourself?

4. If not, why not?

5. If you did an inventory of the people who surround you, such as friends, relatives, or fellow workers, would you classify them as being negative or positive?

6. What would you like to give yourself as a reward for a job well done?

7. What are some of the methods that you are presently using to relax?

8. Do you find that your mind is constantly preoccupied with negative thoughts?

9. If so, why?

You now have learned the tactics used by the street smart sales pros for overcoming their fears, anxieties, and frustrations. If one technique does not work for you, you now have the ability to try another. Street smart sales pros know that it is impossible to eliminate all their fears. If you, too, understand this and are able to deal with your fears on a level that still allows you to achieve positive things, then you have taken a large step towards becoming a street smart sales pro! In addition, the skills found in this chapter go beyond selling. Learning to like yourself will not only reflect upon the way you feel, but will also have a profound effect on who you are as a person and the way you interact with family and friends. It's only street smart to go for it!

11

Handling Objections

An objection is a point made by a prospect that stops him from making a positive decision to purchase. How you handle your prospect's objections can make the difference between making the sale or not.

Inexperienced sales reps as well as underachievers fear customer objections because they do not have the skills to handle them. They lack the understanding as to why customers will use objections before they will commit to purchase, no matter how badly the customers want a product or service.

On the other hand, if you look closely into the eyes of a street smart sales pro right after he hears a client's objection to buy, you undoubtedly will notice a star-like glimmer. This glimmer is there not because he's crazy, although believe me, these savvy sales pros are crazy like foxes. This glimmer is there because he knows that objections can end up being his best friend on a sales call.

The street smart sales pro understands that when a prospect voices an objection, it is a signal that there is interest. This prospect is crying out for help and support. What he is saying is, "I'm not sold yet, but if you can convince me on this point, I might be." This is all a street smart sales pro asks, to be in front of a prospect with interest. He knows it is his job to overcome any objections that his client might have. And these expert sales pros work hard in developing their skills to handle customer concerns.

If you have a prospect who is constantly nodding his head in agreement, never voicing an objection, don't start planning on spending that commission check just yet. You could be in deep trouble. Often, there is little interest when a prospect is nodding in agreement with every point that you are making. Many times what he is actually thinking to himself is, "When is this guy going to be finished? Why did I agree to this appointment?" Finally, when you ask him to purchase, his nod changes to a shake of his head, which emphatically indicates that there is no way that he is ever going to buy from you. Underachievers become discouraged and depressed. After all, they thought that sale was like money in the bank, only it turned out to be a bounced dream!

If you do not presently get a glimmer in your eyes when you hear a prospect's objections to purchase, then it is time that you develop the street smart skills to handle objections. Be street smart, read and study this chapter carefully; it will teach you how to turn your prospect's objections into your best friend!

Why Prospects Object

Did you ever wonder why an individual would object to purchase when he gave all indications that he really wanted and needed your product or service? Often, lacking a valid objection, these individuals will come up with all kinds of ridiculous excuses not to buy. Do you believe these kinds of prospects enjoy giving sales pros a hard time by throwing barriers and obstacles into your path, trying to hamper your efforts to sell them?

Some prospects do enjoy giving a sales pro a hard time. But more often than not, this is not the case. It is more of a state of mind as to why individuals choose to make up all sorts of excuses not to buy. The better you understand their reasoning, the easier it will be for you to overcome their objections to successfully complete the sale. I believe there are four categories of buyers to be aware of.

■ THE PANICKY BUYER

Many individuals find it difficult to make a decision. I have an aunt who practically has a nervous breakdown every time she has to make a decision, and I mean any decision. I've bought houses in less time than it takes her to decide if she is going to have Cheerios or Rice Krispies for breakfast.

There are a lot of people just like my aunt. When they are faced with a situation that calls for a decision, they will begin to perspire as though they were sitting in the middle of a desert. Many times these individuals will blink incessantly and avoid eye contact. If they should happen to be with someone else when they are asked to make a decision, they will constantly ask their companion, "What do you think?"

When selling to these types of individuals, it is even more essential that they feel a strong bond with you than your typical prospect. These individuals must believe that you are out for their best interests. They have to be constantly reassured of this fact. This can be accomplished by making statements that indicate empathy on your part, such as: "I know how you feel, I have felt the same way myself." By doing this, you will make them feel more secure in doing business with you. And that's the street smart bottom line.

■ THE UNBELIEVING BUYER

I know you may find this hard to believe, but some people do not trust salespeople. These prospects keep their guards up in order to avoid being cheated. Knowing this, you have to pay careful attention to what your prospect is saying. This will insure that you will be able to satisfactorily answer any of the objections that he might bring up. You must never gloss over or avoid addressing a prospect's questions or objections. You might believe that you are real slick by avoiding some of his objections, thinking that your prospect has forgotten what he had asked you.

Take this advice to the bank: Prospects do not forget anything. When you don't answer his objections or questions, your prospect feels that you are trying to hide something from him. If you don't know the answer to one of your prospect's questions, tell him you don't. The worst thing that you can do is make up some story that is pure bull. Upon hearing some cockamamie story, a prospect will shut you off faster than you can say, "No sale." There is nothing to be ashamed or embarrassed about for not knowing an answer to a customer's question. Tell him it's a great question. Build up his ego. Reassure him that you will get back to him with the proper information. He will respect your honesty.

In order to build trust, street smart sales pros will repeat a prospect's thoughts and answers. This indicates to your customer that you are paying complete attention to her. You are concerned with what he is saying. Customers are so used to sales pros talking full blast that they immediately respond positively to this approach, which helps to build trust and rapport.

Think before you respond to one of your prospect's questions. Too quick an answer indicates that you don't think too much of the question, or even more important, that you don't think too much of the person asking the question. After answering an objection, make sure before moving on in your presentation that you have answered his question to his satisfaction.

> Ed, it's important for me to answer all my clients' questions to their satisfaction. Have I answered all your questions to your satisfaction?

If your prospect indicates that you have indeed answered his questions or objections, then you have taken a major step in building trust between the two of you. Prospects buy from sales pros whom they trust. On the other hand, if your prospect indicates that you haven't answered all his questions to his liking, ask him specifically what was not answered.

> Lewis, I'm sorry I didn't answer all your questions. Tell me which ones I missed and what additional information you need to know.

Be street smart—answer all your prospect's questions and objections; if you don't know the answers, admit it, it is the street smart thing to do!

■ I'M NOT AN EASY MARK

Some individuals throw out objections even when they know deep down that they are going to buy. They do this because they do not want to look like an easy mark to their salespeople, friends, colleagues, or family. Think about it. Very often, when you speak to people who have made purchases, they will say that they bought the best and at the lowest price. Ironically, many times individuals will boastfully say this even when they know that they have gotten ripped off. People just don't like to admit that they have been taken; they want to save face.

Additionally, people will throw obstacles into your path because they don't want to hear it from a boss, colleague, friend, or wife—or even worse, a mother- and father-in-law—that they were a chump, a salesperson's dream. And if they had gone shopping with any of the above, they most certainly would have gotten a much better deal.

Prospects who feel this way will come up with all sorts of ridiculous excuses not to buy, testing your patience to the limit. Do not become too frustrated or discouraged. Hear them out. Answer all their objections, no matter how nonsensical they may sound. In many instances, after they feel that they have put up sufficient buyer resistance, they will turn around and do what they always wanted to do in the first place.

■ PROSPECTS NEED TO KNOW

Many times prospects object simply because they were not supplied with enough information to buy. Underachievers who do not listen carefully to their prospects rarely discover what their customers' needs, wants, interests, or concerns are; as a result, underachievers are not able to supply their customers with enough meaningful information that will indicate the benefits of purchasing their products or services.

A well-planned presentation can help you avoid this problem. Underachievers who do not have well-planned presentations often will omit important information, which can be confusing to their prospects. And when prospects are confused, they will offer all sorts of opposition to purchase.

Be street smart—give your prospect all the information that she needs to purchase, and do it in a manner that she understands.

Rules for Handling Objections

There are basic rules that you must follow if you are going to successfully answer a prospect's objections. Follow these rules carefully and I guarantee that you will be cashing those large commission checks, which can be very rewarding.

■ DON'T ASSUME ANYTHING

Street smart sales pros do not assume what their prospects might be trying to say. If a prospect makes a statement and they are not absolutely sure what he means, these savvy sales pros are smart enough to ask for more information. Sales pros lose more sales by making wrong assumptions as to what their prospects are trying to convey.

● "Bruce, for my own edification, are you making this purchase as an investment or for pleasure?"

● "Mr. Jones, I'm not entirely sure what you mean by your statement; could you please give me more information?"

Remember, you do not want to spend your time justifying or struggling to answer an objection that does not exist in your customer's mind. Even worse, by wrongly assuming what your prospect is interested in, there is a good chance that you might be ignoring points that are truly important to him, which will surely cost you the sale.

Be street smart—if you are not sure what your prospect has in mind, ask him to restate his question, clarifying the points that you are not sure of. Don't assume anything; if you do, you might as well assume that you are not going to make the sale!

■ NEVER CRITICIZE A PROSPECT'S PREVIOUS DECISION

Street smart sales pros know never to put down a product or service that the prospect is currently using without asking the right questions first. They hold their tongue because they simply do not know how the decision was made to use the competition's product or service. It could have been based on an immediate need, on a solid sales pitch, or it could have taken weeks for the prospect to arrive at that decision. When asking the prospect what firm she has used in the past, some sales reps will wait for the answer and immediately begin to tell the prospect what a terrible choice he made—in essence telling them, "Your choice sucked!"

When this happens, the prospect's face changes and his tone becomes defensive. Instead of working with him, these sales reps have put up a wall between themselves and the prospect that they now have to climb over.

Instead of criticizing the prospect's selection, ask him, "How has that worked out for you?" His answer to that question will provide you with the direction your follow up questions should take. If he says he is not pleased, ask why. If he says he is pleased, ask what he likes about his current firm. Street smart sales pros avoid digging holes for themselves that they can fall into.

■ DON'T WIN THE BATTLE AND LOSE THE WAR!

In a similar manner, sales pros who argue with their clients do not remain in sales very long. Even if you know for certain that your prospect is dead wrong about an issue, you still should avoid getting into a disagreement with him. If you do, it will be the surest way of killing any of your chances of making a sale. Conflict is not productive; you may win the argument, but you'll lose the deal, and most likely the prospect, too.

Instead, encourage the prospect to express his concerns. When you know exactly what his objections are, you'll be better equipped to address them. Be fair, be empathetic. Put yourself in his shoes, and use language that reflects your willingness to relate: "I can see why you might think that," or "I've had clients with similar questions in the past." If the prospect thinks you're on his side, he'll be more likely to listen to what you have to say. Above all, stay calm—by refusing to get into a fight, you remain in control of the situation.

Often, an obstinate client can be overcome with third-party stories. Third-party stories allow you to make a point indirectly, without bullying your client or backing him into a corner. Third-party stories illustrate how another customer benefited from making a deal with you, or, conversely, suffered from declining to use your product or service. They replace conflict with empathy, and help you build an emotional relationship with your client. For more information on third-party stories, see page 161. Be street smart—defuse conflict with empathy and third-party stories!

■ WHEN TO HANDLE AN OBJECTION

Street smart sales pros know that the best time to answer a prospect's objection is immediately. The worst thing you can do is try to gloss over or avoid answering his objection altogether.

By responding quickly to a prospect's objection, you are telling him that you care about him, you are listening to what he has to say. This builds trust and rapport between you and your prospect, which will go a long way towards making the sale.

If you do not immediately answer what is on your prospect's mind, the only thing that he will be thinking about during your sales presentation is why the heck you didn't answer his question. A prospect who is not concentrating on you, as well as on your product or service, will be one impossible prospect to sell. After answering his question, and before you move on with your presentation, make sure his objection is answered to his satisfaction. Get an agreement before continuing.

Sales pro: Manuel, do you now see how you will benefit from this?

Customer: Now I do.

Be street smart—don't put off for later what you can answer right now; for if you do delay, it just might cost you later.

Tactics for Handling Objections

It is critical that you learn to handle objections properly if you are to become a street smart sales pro who earns those large commission checks. This is the area where we separate the achievers from the underachievers. If you are able to answer your prospect's objections to his satisfaction, you should then be able to move smoothly into the final stage of your sales call, which is the close.

Underachievers handle customer objections as if they were trying to do ballet in work boots. They are awkward and clumsy. Handling objections does not mean that you try to outsmart your prospect by some slick flim-flam response to his question or objection. That is not the case.

Handling objections means that you are able to gain the confidence of your prospect by answering his concerns in a logical and convincing manner. The tactics that I have provided for you in this section are based on years of experience in handling prospects' objections successfully. Read, study, and practice these tactics; before long you will be doing perfect pirouettes!

■ THE TACTIC OF QUESTIONING AND LISTENING

The street smart sales pro is keenly aware that there isn't a better technique for uncovering and answering customer objections than the questioning process. The street smart sales pro knows that when he is at the top of his game, closing a high percentage of sales, it is because he is asking the right questions and listening ever so carefully to his customer's responses. Only through this process of asking questions and listening to his prospect's answers can the street smart sales pro truly determine what is important to his customers. And that's the key: Questions help to get your prospect talking in such a manner that he either ends up selling himself or gives you enough information whereby you have the ammunition to overcome any of his concerns.

There are five different kinds of questions that a street smart sales pro uses in order to overcome customer objections. Read, study, and practice using these questioning tactics. You will be pleasantly surprised how much easier it will be for you to handle your prospects' objections in the future.

"Why" Questions

Street smart sales pros use "why" questions in order to get a better understanding as to why their prospects feel a certain way. The following examples will illustrate my point:

Prospect: I'm not interested.

Sales pro: Why do you feel that way?

By using "why" questions and sounding sincere and concerned, there is an excellent chance that you will discover the real reason as to what is holding back your prospect from purchasing. Once you have learned what is holding your prospect back, you will be in a position to handle his concerns. Until then you will be dealing with irrelevant excuses.

Information Questions

Street smart sales pros use questions in order to get new information. Often, this will help to inform you if circumstances that would either help or hurt your chances of making a sale have changed:

- "Glen, are you still having delivery problems?"
- "Fred, are you still using the same supplier for all your widgets?"
- "Is Mr. Curtis still in charge of purchasing?"

Use these types of questions. You can never have too much information. Give your prospects a chance of telling you how things are—it's the street smart thing to do.

Other Concern Questions

This type of question helps the street smart sales pro get additional information by allowing his prospect to discuss any other concerns that he has not voiced.

> Trish, are there any other concerns or reasons that you have in mind, in addition to the one you already mentioned, for not wanting to purchase?

In many instances, prospects will not resent questions phrased this way. Quite often you will discover that your prospect will then give you additional concerns that she has for refusing to buy. At this point you will have a clear picture as to what you are up against.

Open-Ended Questions

Open-ended questions are those that are designed to encourage his prospect to speak freely about a topic of his interest.

Sales pro: You said before that you have had some problems. Could you tell me about them?

Prospect: Well, for the past three years, we have been losing about 10 percent of our customer base because of poor quality control. Not only that, but our costs keep going up, etc.

This type of question is also helpful to the sales pro when he is confronted with a customer who has a tendency to go off on tangents. Commonly, prospects begin to talk about subjects that have nothing to do with the purpose of the call or visit. With this type of question the street smart sales pro can regain control of the sales call, bringing his prospect's attention back to the subject at hand. The open-ended question stimulates the customer to give added information on something already stated.

These kinds of questions are especially effective when you are trying to gather information from a client who may have trouble expressing himself. Open-ended questions require thought on your prospect's part.

Closed-ended Questions

The street smart sales pro uses closed-ended questions in order to steer the conversation toward a specific topic of his choosing and limit his customer's responses mostly to short answers.

Sales pro: Are you having problems increasing your customer base?

Prospect: Yes, I am.

You will find that this questioning tactic can be used for any given situation. The more you practice using questions, the more comfortable and effective you will become. If a client says, "I'm not interested," from now on you will ask, "What seems to concern you?" If a client says, "This is more then I am willing to spend," you will ask, "How much do you want to spend?" If your client says, "You're the best damn sales rep I have ever met," you thank him and ask, "What do you like about me?"

By listening carefully to his client's responses, the street smart sales pro gathers valuable information that makes it easier for him to handle customer objections. Often a prospect will give you so much information that you will be able to overcome his objections by saying, "Based on what you've said . . . ," which is just about the most effective way of getting a client to commit to purchase. After all, if a prospect makes a statement, it is a fact; if you as a sales pro make the same statement, it is considered a sales pitch.

In addition to giving you valuable information, responding to a prospect with a question will also provide you with valuable time in which you can collect your thoughts. During this time, you can map out an intelligent strategy to successfully answer whatever objection that your prospect brings up. Begin to use phrases such as:

- "What do you think?"
- "Why do you ask?"
- "What is your opinion?"
- "How does it appear to you?"

The street smart sales pro uses this questioning technique so often that when someone happens to ask him how he feels, he responds, "How should I feel?" Use this questioning tool; it will effectively help you to answer whatever objections that your prospect might come up with. More importantly, by using a few well-placed questions, you are always in control of your presentation, leading it in the direction that you want it to take.

Be street smart, question everything; your questions will provide you with all the right sales answers!

■ PRODUCT COMPARISON

As I stated in Chapter 8, it is extremely important for you to know the strengths and weaknesses of your products as well as your competitor's products.

If you find that your prospect's decision to buy hinges on a comparison of your product with a competitor's product, it is essential that you be aware of all the advantages and disadvantages of each. If a prospect indicates that your products or services are more expensive than your competitor's, only if you have a clear understanding of why they are more expensive will you be able to turn a negative concern into a positive benefit for your client to purchase. The increased cost may be attributed to a higher quality of material that goes into the manufacturing of your product, which in the long term will prove to be the better purchase for your client.

On the other hand, if you are not familiar with the competition's product or service, you have an excellent opportunity to learn a good deal about your competition by asking your prospect what it is that he that likes or dislikes about the product.

With the right product knowledge you have an opportunity to either compare your product's benefits against the competition or capitalize on your competitor's weaknesses. This can only be done if you have strong product knowledge; being able to point out all the unique strengths of your products or services could make the difference between making the sale or not.

■ GUARANTEES

A primary concern of many prospects is that they are getting taken by you or your company. One of the best tools that you have for relieving this kind of anxiety and concern is your company's or manufacturer's guarantee. If your product or service comes with a guarantee, use it to overcome your prospect's objection to purchase. A guarantee tells your prospect that he is getting exactly what you have promised he would get, without having to take your word for it.

Often, by going over your contract and indicating how it protects the buyer, you will find that much of your prospect's resistance to purchase will disappear.

■ THIRD-PARTY STORIES

A sales rep who does not have a whole bunch of third-party stories is severely limiting his chances of making sales.

As I wrote earlier in the chapter, third-party stories are an excellent way to indirectly make a point in order to overcome the objections of a stubborn customer. A third-party story describes another individual who was in a situation similar to that of your client, and illustrates how that person either profited from your product or service, or suffered from missing the opportunity to purchase it. Depending upon the point that you wish to make, you can guide your story in whichever direction will hit home the hardest with your customer.

Third-party stories turn conflict into clarity; they demonstrate that you are on your client's side, and only want the best for her. The following example will illustrate how effective a third-party story can be in this situation:

> James, about three months ago I was with a client much like your-self, who also believed that upgrading his system was a waste of money. Even though it was against my better judgment, I went along with his thinking, although I knew I should have given him a lot more pressure to convert over. I didn't want him to think that I was trying to sell him something that he didn't need. To make a long story short, because he refused to upgrade, his system had a total breakdown, costing him thousands of extra dollars, not including all the downtime that he experienced. Looking back, I sincerely wish that I had given him more pressure; I'd hate to see that happen to you.

By using a third-party story such as this one, you are able to make a strong point without attacking your prospect's position or ego. Basically, you are telling your prospect that he would have to be a real putz if he didn't learn from this other fellow's misfortune. In many cases, this helps bring your prospect around without causing any fireworks.

Third-party stories can also be effectively used to shed light on an aspect of the prospect's needs that the prospect hadn't considered.

> Elliot, I recently had an opportunity to save one of my customers a good deal of money by selling him my company's product/service. He didn't even realize how much he was losing with the system he had in place! Here's what happened . . .

Third-party stories help you to create positive emotional responses from your prospect—the feelings of opportunity, excitement, or inspiration. They allow you to motivate your customer to improve her own situation or business—by buying your product or service, of course.

Be street smart; have third-party stories available in your selling skills bag. They will lead to many diplomatic sales.

■ "BUT" TACTIC

This is a simple tactic that can be used to give your prospect a bit more information without getting into a confrontation with him.

- "Evan, I can appreciate what you are saying, *but* if you would consider this new bit of information it just might make you change your mind."

- "Wallace, I understand the point that you are trying to make, *but* consider this."

Be street smart, use this tactic; it can help you get another shot at a prospect who may be an obstinate pain in the butt!

Consider This

As you now have learned, answering objections does not mean that you have to use a lot of fast talk in order to convince your prospect that he should buy from you. If you ask the wrong questions, you will never get the right answer. So be street smart—ask the right questions in order to get the right answers, for they will enable you to successfully overcome many of your prospect's objections to purchase. And the next time someone asks you how you feel, ask them, "How should I feel?"

The following eight questions are designed to get you to think like a street smart sales pro with respect to answering customer objections. Read these questions, think about them carefully, and answer them on a sheet of paper.

1. Do you consider your prospect's objections your best friend on a sales call?

2. If not, why not?

3. What are the most frequent objections that you come across?

4. Which objection do you have the most difficulty overcoming?

5. Why?

6. Do you use the questioning technique in trying to overcome customer objections?

7. If not, why not?

8. Specifically, how would you use the following types of questions when encountering customer objections?

    a. Why questions

    b. Information questions

    c. Additional questions

    d. Open-ended questions

    e. Closed-ended questions

Now that you have completed this chapter, you should have a much better understanding as to how to answer your prospect's objections. If you still feel that your prospect's objections are your own worst enemy, then I suggest that you reread this chapter carefully, practice the skills to handle objections, or think about another profession that will not give you as much anxiety. However, if you feel that your new best friend happens to be your prospect's objections, then you have taken a quantum leap towards becoming a street smart sales pro!

12

Closing

The close is a salesperson's ultimate power tool. When used correctly, it provides the means by which the street smart sales pro is able to influence a prospect into making a positive decision in her favor. Closing is the culmination of all the preparation and work that the street smart sales pro has put into her training. It is this critical point in a sales call that the sales pro has been moving towards. Only when she gets a prospect to say, "Yes, I will do business with you," is the sales considered closed, and that is the bottom line for these apt sales pros; everything else is meaningless.

Street smart sales pros know only too well that companies do not pay commission to salespeople who try hard and almost make the sale. "Almost" sales do not pay the mortgage, "almost" sales do not buy you all the wonderful toys that are available. Only signed contracts or purchase orders from customers who want to use your products or services have any worth.

Knowing that the only way that they can earn big bucks is to bring in a purchase order, street smart sales pros are relentless in their pursuit to close the deal. The very first moment that a street smart sales pro meets her prospect, she has only one thought in mind: to concentrate her efforts to get the job done; to close that sale!

There is nothing more challenging to the street smart sales pro than having the ability to influence a prospect to make a positive decision in her favor; when she does, this skillful achiever experiences an exhilarating high that motivates her to persevere until she is able to close the next deal.

The closing tactics of the fakers, takers, and makers are so limited that it becomes virtually impossible for these underachievers to close their sales successfully on a consistent basis. Their closing attempts are often awkward, clumsy, inappropriate, and amateurish, making it quite easy for their prospects to reject their offerings. At times, these under-achievers are so ill at ease or embarrassed in a closing situation that they even become hesitant to ask for the order.

Underachievers are not professional closers; they do not consis-tently get the job done. When they close a sale, more often than not it is out of chance rather than as a result of their sales skills. Prospects more likely buy products or services from these fakers, takers, and makers because they have an imminent need of what these reps have to offer, not because of their skill at selling.

If you are a salesperson who suffers from sweaty palms associated with closing, causing you to be uncomfortable and hesitant to ask for the order, it is time that you develop strong, sound, money-making street smart closing tactics. This chapter will provide you with loads of clever, effective, and proven closes for becoming a professional street smart closer. These tactics are the ones being utilized daily by those who have achieved enormous success by consistently closing their sales. Become street smart; read carefully and get the job done!

The Street Smart Chameleon

Street smart sales pros are not lucky when they sell to a customer; nobody can be consistently lucky. They have a high closing rate because they have in their bag of selling skills a number of effective closing techniques that enable them to persuasively convince their prospects to purchase. These clever sales pros have many options when they close, never having to be dependent on one or two tactics; if they were, they certainly would not be able to handle all the vari-ous customer personalities and sales situations that they encounter in the real world of selling. Street smart sales pros understand that there is no one magical close that works every time. Even if they have had success with a particular closing tactic nine straight times, they are aware that this tactic just might not cut it the tenth time. Street smart sales pros always prepare themselves for that tenth time, the unexpected situation!

Throughout this chapter, we will discuss in detail the different kinds of closes that you can use in your day-to-day selling. Street smart sales pros are successful because they have the ability to recognize which specific closing technique to use in order to motivate and convince their prospects to buy.

Street smart sales pros also have the ability to adapt to the personalities of their prospects, which helps these versatile sales pros build trust and rapport between themselves and their clients. This is essential if you are to become a consistent closer.

Underachievers do not adapt their selling techniques to anyone; they treat all their customers as if they had the same personality. It is no wonder that they do not close consistently, losing many opportunities to earn those large commission checks. Instead of realizing that they are not connecting on a personal level with their clients, they blame their lack of success on their prospects, accusing them of just shopping around and not really being interested in buying.

Street smart sales pros know that if they don't connect with their prospects, they have no one to blame but themselves, so they work hard to connect. They want the big bucks, and like chameleons, these savvy sales pros are able to adapt to their prospects' personalities. Street smart sales pros can be comical, serious, creative, straightforward, haughty, or down and dirty. Whatever it takes, these achievers have the strategy to relate to their clients.

■ SERIOUS STREET SMART CHAMELEON TACTICS

If a street smart sales pro finds herself selling a prospect who is serious and not interested in small talk, she makes sure that she does not go off on a tangent; she sticks close to her presentation and answers all her customer's questions in a clear and forthright manner.

A tactic used by the street smart sales pro when faced with this solemn type of client is to slow down her speech, pausing every so often, projecting a feeling that she is giving deep consideration to her prospect's needs and concerns. In addition, she keeps her posture erect, never slouching, which would convey a more relaxed, informal, and less serious mood.

By using these tactics, you will discover that prospects with sober personalities will relate to you. And if they relate to you, they'll buy from you—which is the bottom line!

■ OUTGOING STREET SMART CHAMELEON TACTICS

On the other hand, if a street smart sales pro finds herself in front of a prospect who is open, friendly, or quick to laugh, our artful chameleon becomes Ellen DeGeneres (or Jon Stewart, if he's a man), greatly enhancing her chances of successfully closing the sale.

A less formal presentation is the tactic used by the street smart sales pro in selling to a client with this type of personality. Small talk can be used, while you attentively listen and observe the subjects that might be of interest to your customer, such as discussing sports, your client's children, or a particular piece of jewelry that she may be wearing. On these occasions it is a good idea to have one or two good jokes tucked away.

Your posture is not formal; crossing your legs, as well as supporting your smiling face in your hands, is perfectly okay. Statements like, "You are one fun guy," "You must have been some wild kid growing up," said in a laughing tone, sometimes will help you connect with these types of clients.

For some salespeople, humor is not something that comes easily to them. I knew a very successful caterer who knew how to change his presentation based on the type of prospect sitting in front of him. He would search the Internet for jokes. He would write down and memorize the best of the batch. He would then keep a sheet of paper with just the punch lines on his desk in front of him, and when he thought he needed to interject a little humor, he was ready. He made sure to keep the jokes related to the type of parties his customers were inquiring about and never questionable in taste.

So whether it's the prospect initiating the humor or you, remember, not to get so relaxed that you are not concentrating on the reason that you are there, to close the deal; that's the bottom line; no kidding!

Now that you understand the importance of adapting to the personality of your client, use these street smart tactics to make a connection.

If you find it is not in your personality to adapt to different types of people, closing consistently will be a problem for you. But, if you can become a chameleon, you have taken a giant step towards becoming a successful street smart closer!

Trial Close

A trial close is used by the street smart sales pro in order to test the waters; it gives her an indication as to how positive or negative her prospect may be at a certain point in her presentation. The advantage of using trial closes is that they afford you the flexibility of asking for the order without risking a halt to your presentation.

In most cases, a prospect will not cut you off completely by giving you a simple "no" when she indicates that she is not going to buy; on many occasions, she will tell you the definite reason why she is hesitant to commit to purchase. This gives the street smart sales pro an opportunity to concentrate on her client's area of concern, directing her presentation where the emphasis is most needed. She simply states, "Brian, I get so excited talking about my product, sometimes I forget to give my customers all the pertinent information, and that's just what I did with you. Of course you can't make a positive decision based on what I've told you." This allows our street smart sales pro to continue her sales call, but with a renewed emphasis on the areas in which the prospect has concerns. Notice how smart she was when she told the prospect that as soon as he gets all the relevant information he would then be able to make a positive decision.

On the other hand, when you use a trial close, your prospect may give you every indication that he is ready to buy. If that be the case, forget the rest of your presentation and go right for the close.

Listed below are some examples of how a street smart sales pro phrases a trial close:

- "Nick, are you buying for investment or pleasure?"

- "Would you want the red widgets or the blue ones?"

- "When we start working with you, you'll quickly see the difference in service."

- "I hope I can squeeze you in as soon as next week."

After you have made one of these statements, the client might either give you an indication of agreement, or simply respond that she has not made up her mind just yet as to whether she is going to go with you. If you have used this trial close early in your presentation, you can use the example that I gave you above to continue the sales call. She indeed needs more information before making a positive decision to go with you. On the other hand, if the trial close is used at the end and you do not get a "yes," simply ask "Gee, Mary, what are the concerns that are holding you back from making a positive decision?" Wait for her answer. She most likely will give you the information that you need to use to try to overcome his concern.

All sales pros should practice using trial closes; they help to condition your prospects into saying "yes." If you wait until the very end of your presentations to try to get a commitment, you are putting too much pressure on the decision-making capabilities of your clients.

Emotional Appeal Selling

Street smart sales pros realize that in many instances individuals purchase what they want based on emotion, not necessarily what they need based on logic. When people choose to buy expensive pieces of jewelry, they do so not because they need the jewelry in order to survive, but because, emotionally, buying it makes them feel good. Street smart sales pros work hard to discover just what an individual's emotional needs are, and as soon as they determine them, they work extremely hard to satisfy these needs. This allows the street smart sales pros to close many a profitable deal.

The following examples will indicate to you just how many different types of emotional closes there are; after all, as individuals we are emotional animals, motivated by many different factors. These various closes will give you an idea how emotional selling can be a useful tactic for closing a sale.

■ THE EGO CLOSE

I know a very successful exotic-car saleswoman. On many occasions she has told me that if her customers bought strictly on logic she would never make a sale. After all, how practical is it to drive a car that cost $100 thousand to the local mall?

Knowing the reasons why her customers buy is an enormous help to her when she goes for the close.

The initial tactic that she uses when a prospect shows interest in a particular automobile is to get her behind the wheel for a test drive. As understanding that image is important to her clients, she issues sporadic but well-planned statements such as: "Mr./Mrs./Ms. _____, you look fantastic behind that wheel; that car is really you;" "I don't know what kind of business you're in, but obviously you have to be successful to be considering a luxury car of this magnitude. Doesn't it make you feel as if you are out in front of a parade?;"and, "Not too many people are fortunate enough to own a luxury car such as this, you must be real proud of yourself." (Notice how she uses the phrase "luxury car," never just "car;" this adds a snob appeal to her product.)

By the time her client has finished road testing that particular automobile, she feels an emotional need to own it. Logic doesn't come into play, allowing our street smart saleswoman to earn many large commission checks.

This street smart auto saleswoman was able to create an image of what owning the car would mean to her prospect on an emotional level, allowing her heart instead of her head to make the decision to purchase.

■ "DON'T YOU CARE?" CLOSE

The street smart sales pro creates an emotional image in the mind of her prospect, such that if she doesn't take action to purchase, she will be negatively affecting her loved ones. This tactic is based on the fact that most people find it a lot easier to say no if they believe it might only affect themselves; they do not feel real comfortable gambling with their loved ones' lives.

> Ellen, it is true that this safety feature will further add to your costs; but if your loved ones are ever in an accident, it will most likely save their lives. Isn't that worth the added cost?

Can you imagine what it would take for this prospect to say the safety of his family just isn't worth the added cost, especially if her husband and kids are present? For that prospect to say no, either she would have to be one heartless person, or planning on taking the first plane out of the country.

This tactic can be used when selling any kind of products for the home, car, or workplace, in which safety plays a part. When used appropriately, it can be a major factor in shifting a prospect's view.

■ THE INTANGIBLE FANTASY CLOSE

In the intangible fantasy close, street smart sales pros are able to paint a picture of what a prospect would hope to have one day. And they know how to paint—they are the Picassos of word images. By the time the street smart sales pro is finished creating her word images, her prospects can vividly picture their dreams right before their eyes. This tactic is especially effective because fantasies are a lot more majestic, fun, and less costly than reality.

> Mrs. Smith, can you see how beautiful your home will look over there on that knoll? Are you going to have large windows so you can take advantage of that magnificent panoramic view? Imagine you and your family waking up to that sunrise every morning. What a great way to start your day!

This street smart sales pro created a vision of a home that not only is not there, but may never be built. She created hope and dreams for her prospect. Her use of visual imagery conjured up all sorts of positive emotional feelings on the part of her customer. Anybody selling an intangible item can generate pictures that might be far more exciting or alluring than the reality, and this will lead to sales.

■ "REST ASSURED" CLOSE

By using this tactic, the sales pro is able to create an emotional image in the mind of her prospect, convincing her that she no longer will have to twist and turn at night worrying about a particular aspect of his life. In the pressured world that we live in today, individuals appreciate and are willing to pay in order to "rest assured" about a particular concern.

> This insurance policy will see that your children are provided for in case of your death. Isn't peace of mind worth the added premium, knowing that their educational needs are going to be taken care of?

The street smart sales pro is creating a feeling in her prospect's mind that if anything happens to her, she can rest assured that her children will be provided for. This tactic can be used by anyone who is offering a product or service that will give a feeling of peace of mind. Here's how an attorney would use this tactic.

> If you do not spend the money now to update your contracts, insuring that they are foolproof and will protect you as well as your company, you may wake up one day without the company that you worked so hard to build. Isn't it worth the added cost to rest assured that this will never happen?

In summary, street smart sales pros are able to size up their prospects on an emotional level. They never assume what motivates them to buy. These proficient sales pros are aware that there will be times when a customer will initially talk about price, price, price; but after further investigation, the street smart sales pro will discover that the customer has emotional wants and needs, which often take precedence over price. Street smart sales pros also understand that the more they can create emotional satisfaction for their prospects, the higher the price their customers will be willing to pay and the easier the close. Be street smart—don't always sell to the head; after all, the heart is where the "rest assured" sale lies!

Quality Selling

Quality selling is based on the fact that your products or services are really good and, in many instances, are superior to your competition's. Street smart sales pros like to sell the quality of their product or service. They know that then their prospects will not be as price conscious and will be willing to overlook higher cost or later deliveries.

The quality, puppy dog, inventory, and Ben Franklin closes are used by street smart sales pros in order to get their prospects to purchase based on the quality of their products or services.

■ QUALITY CLOSE

The quality close is based on the premise that people are really interested in quality when they make a purchase. Individuals may want to buy cheap, but street smart sales pros know they do not want to buy garbage.

Sales pro: Cassandra, I cannot lower my price any further, and the reason for that is based entirely on the fact that my company made a commitment to clients like yourself.

Customer: What do you mean?

Sales pro: Many years ago, my company made the decision that it would be much easier to explain price one time only, rather than apologizing for poor quality forever. Knowing this, Cassandra, I am sure you are glad we made that pledge.

What is this prospect going to say—"No, I like buying junk"? The street smart sales pro knows for the most part that her prospects are not going to respond by saying that quality is not important. If you have a quality product or service, tell your prospects about it; it will close sales for you.

■ PUPPY DOG CLOSE

The puppy dog close is utilized by all street smart sales pros who are selling a quality product that can be left behind with a prospect to use for an agreed time and, if not totally satisfied, not be obligated to purchase. The theory behind this close, like the parents who take a puppy dog home for their children and quickly fall in love with the dog, is that once a customer tries your product, she will never consider giving it back.

This can only be done with a superior product that will indeed make prospects want to own it after using it. Obviously, if they have any sort of difficulty with your product or service, they will gladly want you to take it back.

Olivia, why don't I just leave my copying machine here for two weeks. I'm willing to do this because I know our system is superior to anything you have seen or used. Be my guest; if you don't want it after the two weeks, there is no obligation on your part; I will be happy to take it back.

Any sales pro selling a quality product that can be left behind or a service that can be used on a trial basis can use the puppy dog close, relying on the fact that once her prospects get used to their new conveniences they will never want to give them back!

■ BEN FRANKLIN CLOSE

This close is based on a method used by Ben Franklin. Whenever he had an important decision to make, he would take out a piece of paper and divide it into two columns. At the top of one side of the paper he would write "pros," and on the top of the other side of paper he would write "cons." He then would list all the positive reasons and all the negative reasons for making a decision, and when he finished with this exercise, Franklin would see which side outweighed the other.

The street smart sales pro, knowing that the quality of her product will deliver far more benefits than drawbacks, will use this very same exercise in getting her customer to make a decision to purchase. The street smart sales pro first describes how Franklin utilized this two-column process to assure himself that he indeed would make the best decision possible. Then the street smart sales pro has her prospect write down the pros and cons of purchasing her product.

Pros	*Cons*
1. More dependable	1. Price slightly higher.
2. Easier to maintain	
3. Will increase production	
4. Always in stock.	

As you can see for yourself, Andre, the pros certainly outweigh the cons. Look at the benefits that you will derive just by paying slightly more than you are used to. You can see in black and white that the quality will make it less expensive in the long run.

This tactic also gives you an opportunity to hear your customers' concerns, which you then can try to overcome at a later point in the sales call, if they are still holding up your prospect from moving forward.

■ INVENTORY CLOSE

This tactic is used when a prospect indicates that he could get a faster delivery date if he ordered from a competitor. The street smart sales pro's answer is a logical and effective close.

Sales pro: Gabe, what does it tell you about my product that I can't keep enough in stock?

Prospect: It tells me that you don't make enough.

Sales pro: No, Gabe, it tells you because of our superior quality there is a huge demand for our product, that it's a product worth waiting for, and that's why you want it.

The puppy dog, quality, Ben Franklin, and inventory closes give the street smart sales pro an opportunity to make sales based on quality, with less emphasis on price. Street smart sales pros do not want to be the cheapest folks in town; companies do not pay large commissions for that kind of sales approach. Be street smart—sell the quality of your product; it's worth it!

Benefit Selling

Benefit selling is used to indicate to a prospect that the quicker she makes a decision to purchase, the greater the reward to her. Street smart sales pros use this close effectively in order to create urgency on the part of their customers to buy. Urgency, the fear of losing out on an opportunity, is a heck of a motivator; and if the sense of urgency is used effectively, customers will buy.

■ THREE QUESTION BENEFIT CLOSE

The street smart sales pro asks her clients three questions that lead them to the conclusion that the longer they wait to purchase, the more it will cost them. The street smart sales pro words her questions in such a manner that her prospects would appear to be foolish if they did not agree to purchase:

- "Tara, can you see where this would save you money?"

- "Are you interested in saving money?"

- "If you were to become interested in starting to save money, when do you think would be the best time to start?"

Here is another example:

- "Rhea, can you see how this machine will make your factory more efficient?"

- "Are you interested in running a more efficient factory?"

- "When do you think it would be the best time to begin running your factory more efficiently?"

Observe how the street smart sales pro controls where she wants to go in the close. The answers are obvious; and if she should get a negative response, she has a strong, logical chance to overcome any objections that her client may come up with.

■ BENEFIT BY OTHERS' MISFORTUNE CLOSE

This close is based on the fact that individuals love to get bargains, and they especially feel that they made a good deal when they are able to profit from someone else's misfortunes. Aware of this, the street smart sales pro uses this close in the following way:

- "Mrs. Brown, I can give it to you at this price because the other couple just could not keep up their payments. As a result, you will be able to take advantage of what they already put into the deal."

- "This house is worth much more money, but since the owners are going through a difficult divorce, they are willing to let it go for that price. If you move quickly, you can take advantage of this situation."

- "You are really lucky! The only reason this is available is due to the fact that the other people could not get the credit; if you move quickly, you can take advantage of the situation."

This is a fantastic close; when using it you will see how individuals will move quickly once they see how they can benefit from another person's misfortune.

"Give Them What They Want" Selling

"Give them what they want" selling is based on the fact that you have gone through your entire presentation and your prospect has given all indication that your product or service meets his needs and wants and is ready to purchase.

Once the prospect has made the commitment to buy, the street smart sales pro asks for the order in a matter-of-fact manner, using the assumptive and alternate of choice closes. This is important, for if you sound nervous, surprised, or excited when you assume the sale is made, it might scare your prospect into thinking that he has indeed made his decision too quickly.

■ ASSUMPTIVE CLOSE

The assumptive close is used by the street smart sales pro when she has gone through her entire presentation, all along getting positive answers to her trial closes. The street smart sales pro assumes then that it is a natural process for her client to buy and makes a closing statement such as, "Velma, all you have to do is sign here and I will get you immediate delivery," or "Please hand me the phone so I can call in your order."

If your prospect does not object, then your deal is closed without your actually having to ask for a decision on his part.

■ ALTERNATE OF CHOICE CLOSE

An alternate of choice close is based on a sales pro's asking a question that leaves no room for her prospect to indicate anything but that a sale has been made. As in the assumptive close, the street smart sales pro uses this tactic if her prospect has indicated all along that she has no objections to purchasing.

- "Martin, do you want one or two dozen?"

- "Which do you prefer, delivery on Wednesday or Thursday?"

- "Do you want the deluxe model or the super deluxe?"

- "Which do you prefer, ordering the green ones or the blue ones?"

If the client should happen to answer that he is not interested in either choice, as in all closes that may not work, the street smart sales pro then goes through the process discussed in Chapter 11, "Handling Objections," trying to isolate what her prospect's concerns are. Knowledge is more than half the battle when it comes to making a sale.

Price Selling

Street smart sales pros are aware that it is impossible to get top price for their products or services every time. The difference between the underachiever and the street smart sales pro is the fact that the underachiever starts out low in price and goes lower to close her deals, whereas the street smart sales pro starts out at a higher price and, only through negotiations and commitments made by her prospect, chooses to bend her price. She does not discount her price easily, as if it were coming to her customer all along.

The street smart sales pro uses the following tactics when she realizes that she has to negotiate price in order to close a deal. By using these tactics, even though she might have to lower her price, she often is able to obtain an added benefit for herself or her company that will make the deal more palatable. Study and use these tactics; they apply to many different selling situations.

■ MORE FOR LESS PRICE CLOSE

If a street smart sales pro is representing a product that can be purchased in quantities, she offers a lower price based on her prospect's ability to buy in larger amounts.

> Ray, we can agree on this price, all you have to do is buy an extra gross. You drive a hard bargain, but I'll do it.

Notice how the street smart sales pro assumes that her customer will take the extra amount. This is a form of an assumptive close, which we discussed earlier in this chapter.

■ ADD ON PRICE CLOSE

Cash discounts can be offered to customers based on their purchasing additional items that you sell.

> Lisa, I can only sell you this camera for that price as long as you agree to purchase an additional ten rolls of film.

■ CASH AND CARRY PRICE CLOSE

Street smart sales pros can offer discounts to customers who agree to pay on better terms, such as cash on delivery (C.O.D.).

> Lina, it is extremely difficult for me to give you that kind of price. The only way that I can possibly see my way clear to do it is if you agree to pay C.O.D.

■ REFERRAL PRICE CLOSE

Street smart sales pros will lower their price if their customers will recommend other potential clients to them.

> Brenda, I will lower my price on the condition that you will agree to try to refer other customers to me. I know if you agree to this, it will not be an idle promise on your part just to get a special price.

Notice how the street smart sales pro used the words "on the condition that you will agree to this," instead of "the condition that you say you will," which does not carry as strong a commitment. In addition, she reinforces this commitment by indicating that she only agreed to lower her price because she believes her client is a woman of her word. This now makes her client feel emotionally obligated not to go back on her word.

■ IMMEDIACY PRICE CLOSE

Street smart sales pros will give discounts to clients who agree to take immediate delivery.

Paula, I can only give you that kind of deal if you agree to take immediate delivery. If I have to hold it in my warehouse one extra day, I just cannot do it.

■ REDUCE TO THE SMALLEST VARIABLE PRICE CLOSE

The street smart sales pro shrewdly uses this tactic to overcome price objections by breaking down the difference between what her prospect wants to pay and what she wants to sell for into its smallest component. By doing so, the street smart sales pro can get her prospect to understand that what she is arguing so strongly about just isn't that important.

> Ingrid, I know this house has to be sold for $63,000 and that you wanted to spend only $53,000, but based on what you've said, this house is everything you wanted it to be, and you can fully expect to live in it for the next twenty years. The $10,000 difference is what we are talking about; and divided over twenty years, it comes out to less than ten dollars a week. Is that what is going to keep you from purchasing your dream house?
>
> or
>
> Mr. and Mrs. Smith, I know our oil is five cents higher than you are presently paying, but based on what you've said, you would feel more secure for your family by using a full-service oil company, never having to worry about keeping your family warm in the winter. You told me you burn a thousand gallons of oil per year, which comes out to about one dollar a week more than you are currently paying. Knowing all this now, doesn't it make sense to have all this security for only a dollar?

In many instances, the street smart sales pro who uses this tactic is able to get her prospect to realize that it is ridiculous to deny herself the benefits of the product or service.

The key to negotiating price is to make sure that if you have to lower your price, you lower it in such a fashion that your prospect believes he is fortunate to get it. The tactic used by the street smart sales pro is to give in slowly when she negotiates. She also knows to concede in small increments; why give away the store if you don't have to? The street smart sales pro tries to close by splitting the difference as opposed to dropping her price all the way down. But most important, if you agree to lower your price, make sure it is based on the fact that your prospect has committed himself to buy. After giving away the store, many underachievers find out that they still have not made the sale. Be street smart—if you are going to give, make sure you are also going to receive!

Concession Selling

Concession selling is when you have to give up something in order to make a deal. It personally grieves me to give anything away; however, in the real world, street smart sales pros know that we have to do what we have to do. The old saying, "Half a pie is better than no pie at all," relates to this kind of selling, although the street smart sales pro works really hard not to give away a single piece too easily.

■ CONTINGENCY CONCESSION CLOSE

The street smart sales pro restates her offer to her customers so that the decision to purchase is dependent upon some other factors that normally would not be offered.

- "Sandi, if I could get the company to go along with giving you a loaner car, then would you order the car today?"

- "If I can get you an exclusive distributorship for the line, will you take it in by the end of the month?"

■ GIVE AWAY CONCESSION CLOSE

This close happens when the street smart sales pro offers an added incentive to her prospect if he agrees to buy that very moment. This is only offered as the last resort and at the very end of the sales call. The street smart sales pro doesn't want her prospects to think that they can get even more products or services for free.

- "Claire, if you can take six today, I can throw in two extra."

- "If you take delivery of the car today, I can give you free rust proofing."

The important thing to remember when you have to make concessions is to be sure that the deal can actually be made. You don't want to work really hard, losing valuable selling time, only to agree to something that just can't be done. Know what you can give, and give in a fashion whereby your prospect feels she has made the best deal possible.

"Nothing to Lose" Selling

This kind of selling is tried only after you have totally exhausted all other tactics. The nothing to lose selling can be a lot of fun, simply because you can do whatever, because you have nothing to lose! In some instances by being funny, outrageous, or different, you will be surprised by a prospect who will change her negative thinking.

Remember, after you've spent a lot of time with your prospect and are about to leave, you can give it one more college try by using these tactics. Be street smart—have some fun with it; it just might surprise you.

■ NEGATIVE CLOSE

This close is based on the fact that people want things they cannot have. If all else is not working, sometimes a client can be sold when she believes she is going to lose out on an opportunity. When you see you are going nowhere in closing and, in fact, start to feel that you are turning off your client altogether, begin to pack up your materials and say the following:

> Alana, I do not want you to feel like I am shoving my product down your throat. I should never have to do that while promoting this kind of quality product. As a representative of this company for many years, I know that not all people can see the advantages of my product, and as a result, it is not for everybody, and obviously it is not for you.

After making this statement, continue ever so slowly to pack up, and make sure you keep your mouth closed. Often you will hear your customer say, "I didn't say it wasn't for me," whereupon you respond, "Then let's get the deal done." The prospect, seeing that you are taking the opportunity to buy away from her, will often come around and decide to purchase.

■ COLUMBO CLOSE

In the long-running classic television series *Columbo,* actor Peter Falk played a very clever police detective. This close is based on a method used by his character, Lieutenant Columbo. Invariably, as Columbo was about to leave his suspect, giving the criminal false security, he would turn and ask, "Do you mind if I ask you a question?," thereby opening up a full discussion in hopes of getting valuable information.

The street smart sales pro does the same thing. She pretends to be finished with her sales call, actually packing up her materials, which relaxes her prospect and makes her think that the presentation is over; and before she gets up to leave, our savvy sales pro asks:

Sales pro: Do you mind if I ask you one question, Christina?

Customer: Sure, fire away.

Sales pro: Is it the fact that you did not have faith in me and my company that held you up from ordering?

Customer: No, you seem to be an ethical person.

Sales pro: Was it the fact that you thought our price was too high?

Customer: No, your price seemed reasonable.

The street smart sales pro will go on and on, covering all the significant points in her presentation, until she comes across the objection that was not answered satisfactorily, giving her another opportunity to try to overcome it.

On the other hand, if the street smart sales pro goes through all her questions and does not get a negative answer, she simply turns toward her prospect and says, "Christina, if you are so satisfied with everything, why not move forward to secure the goods needed?" At this point, keep your mouth shut and wait for your customer's answer. In many instances the client will give you a "yes" to move forward; but if you should happen to get a "no," you still have a chance to try to discover what his real reason is for holding back from buying. The last tactic used at this point is simply to say, "Christina, I'm leaving; I do not want to pressure you to say 'yes;' that's not my style (make sure you keep a straight and sincere face when you utter these white lies); but for my own edification, why the heck aren't you saying 'yes?' Based upon what you've said, I know you are pleased with the benefits of my product." Again, keep quiet; at this point your client may be worn down and give you the real reason why she does not want to buy, which is all you can hope for.

■ THE ASSERTIVE CLOSE

I do not suggest that you use this close with an ex-football player, but if you read your client as a person who might purchase if you assert yourself, give it a shot. Some prospects like sales pros who are assertive; it shows them you have confidence in yourself as well as your product.

> Lois, I've been coming to see you for three years, and I'm tired of leaving without an order. I don't care how long I have to sit here, I'm not leaving without an order. Once you give me the opportunity to work with you, I know you're going to love to do business with us.

Look right into her eyes when you say that, indicating that you mean business. Sometimes a prospect will throw you a bone just to get rid of you; but by chance if you happen to have misread her and your prospect starts to charge at you with malice in her eyes, it's best to leave.

■ THE POOR SOUL CLOSE

This close is based on the fact that people have hearts and are apt to give a break to someone down on her luck. Remember, don't be depressed by using this close, it is only a tactic, and you are using it because you have nothing to lose!

> Ms. Brown, I'm really new at this, and I'm not sure if you remember when you first got started how hard it was, but all I know is that my product is really good and I know you won't be disappointed. My calling your order in is going to make so much of a difference. I really would appreciate it.

Granted, this close may not be for everyone, but it can be effective and lead to sales. By your following up with this client and indicating how grateful you are for the order, you can develop a strong relationship.

■ "PUH-LEASE" CLOSE

This close can be pretty funny when used in the right situation, especially if you have a sense of humor. Simply put, it is based on the theory of begging—after all, some street smart sales pros are good beggars. When using this close, think of Bambi when he learns that his mom is dead; it helps to create empathy between you and your prospect.

> Puh-lease (What he is saying is please, but if you whine and beg properly, it comes out *puh-lease*) Ms. Brown, give me the order, puh-lease.

Now, you may feel this kind of approach can be degrading or humiliating, and I guess to the average sales pro it is. But not to the street smart sales pro. The sales pro is a fox and will do whatever it takes to make the sale. Remember, the one who laughs last often cashes the largest commission checks. Be street smart—be polite and *puh-lease* ask for the order!

■ THE CARD COMMITMENT CLOSE

The card commitment close is used by the street smart sales pro in order to get a commitment for a future appointment to discuss whatever proposal has been made. The street smart sales pro is aware that she will lose an opportunity to close a sale if she merely hands a prospect her business card without trying to obtain some kind of commitment.

Often, when a prospect asks for your card at the end of your presentation without giving you a positive decision to purchase, she does so more as a polite formality than anything else. Instead of handing her card over and walking away with nothing more than hope, a street smart sales pro would handle it in this fashion:

Sales pro: "Nancy, you obviously want my business card so that we can get together to discuss my proposal at greater lengths, isn't that so?"

Prospect: "Absolutely."

Sales pro: "Terrific. Let me put on the front of my card the time and date of our next appointment. I can see you either Monday or Wednesday of next week (alternate of choice close); which do you prefer?"

If your prospect indicates that he does not want another appointment, you can then start probing again to uncover her concerns and objections. If, on the other hand, she does consent to see you again, you have given yourself another opportunity to close the sale. Use your business card as a sales tool, not merely a giveaway.

If you find that you are still unable to close a particular prospect after trying all the tactics and knowledge that we have discussed, it is at this point that you have to realize that some people just can't be sold. Be street smart—don't be discouraged; move on to your next opportunity.

When to Close

Street smart sales pros try to close as early as possible, knowing that more sales opportunities are missed by sales pros who do not realize that their prospects were indeed ready to buy. As a result, many sales pros talk themselves out of sales by overselling.

We have already learned that through the use of trial closes, the street smart sales pro can test the waters in order to see if her prospect is ready to make a purchase.

The street smart sales pro is constantly watching for clues that will indicate that her prospect is ready to buy.

Through observation, a street smart sales pro may detect her prospect unconsciously giving a favorable nod of her head. Her body may become relaxed, indicating that he has taken the pressure off herself by having made a decision as to what she wants to do. The expressions she makes with her face—a smile or a relaxed forehead—can also indicate to you that she is on your side and is ready to buy.

Street smart sales pros are excellent listeners; they do not want to miss hearing a valuable spoken word that might indicate that their prospect is ready to purchase. Phrases like, "Do you give terms?" "How long is your guarantee?" "This suit makes me feel like a million bucks," are strong indications that it is time to go for the close.

Be street smart; listen and observe. As you gain experience, you will have little trouble picking up these invaluable clues that will tell you if it is time to at least try to close the deal.

When to Stop Closing

When your prospect says "yes"—and she will—stop pitching. Understand that you have accomplished your goal. Many salespeople continue to talk, going on about this and that, seemingly ignoring what they have just achieved. Don't talk out of nervousness, and don't oversell your product! You may say something that may actually turn a "yes" into a "maybe," killing the sale.

Instead, smile, shake the hand of your new customer, and say, "Thank you. I appreciate your business." If your product comes with the offer of an extended warranty, suggest it to the client at this time—otherwise, quit while you're ahead. Don't try to sell the store—the last thing you want to do is push too hard and risk irritating your client. You are building a long-term relationship; what you think you're giving up in immediate sales may result in greater customer fidelity and bigger dividends over the years. Follow up by saying, "If you have any questions, don't hesitate to give me a call." While you may want to whoop and holler at that moment, save your excitement for later. Go back to your office and do your victory dance there!

Consider This

The street smart sales pro knows that all her sales efforts will have gone for naught unless she is able to get her prospect to commit to purchase. This is the only way she can earn those large commissions—closing, getting the job done! The street smart sales pro constantly closes well because she has studied and developed sales tactics that give her the ammunition to overcome client objections.

As you have learned in this chapter, there is a lot more to closing than just asking for the order. Be street smart—learn as many of these techniques as possible and adapt them to your own situation and personality. Only then will you be able to consistently influence your prospects to make decisions in your favor, which is the bottom line!

The following ten questions are designed to see if you are starting to think like a street smart closer. See if you have what it takes to get the job done. Read these questions, consider them carefully, and answer them on a sheet of paper.

1. When you are trying to close a prospect, do you feel you are in control?

2. If not, why not?

3. Do you have a well-planned, thought-out strategy that you can utilize as you get into a closing situation?

4. If not, why not?

5. Do you tend to rely on lowering your price in order to close the sale?

6. If so, why?

7. How many closes do you have, and what are they?

8. Which close would you use to handle each of the following objections made by one of your prospects?

   a. You just have to do better on the price.

   b. There's so much to take into consideration, I'm afraid to make a decision right now.

   c. Everything sounds great; I'll let you know about that money-saving widget next week.

   d. Does this car come in green?

   e. I only wanted to spend $5,000, not $5,500, on my outside deck.

9. Do you utilize trial closes in your presentation?

10. If not, why not?

Now that you have finished reading this chapter, you should realize that street smart sales pros close consistently not because they are lucky—far from it. They close sales because they are prepared. In their bag of selling skills are bundles of closing tactics that enable the street smart sales pros to positively influence their prospects to make decisions to purchase.

If you go through these various techniques and still find that you are uncomfortable closing, selling may not be for you. However, if after studying, practicing, and using these techniques, you have found that your sweaty palms have disappeared, and you have a strong desire to move on to your next potential customer, then congratulations—you have taken your final step towards becoming a street smart sales pro!

Putting It Together

Before I let you go, I'd like to get something off my chest. When I first went into sales, it felt good—no, it felt great—as though it was a role that I was born to play. Now, I'll admit that I was not the world's best student when I was going to school, but I knew I had an innate ability to work with people in a way that allowed me to get the responses I was looking for.

When I worked as a teacher in the South Bronx, my kids were tough cookies. While other teachers had absolutely no control over their classrooms, my students sat in their seats, listened, asked questions, and hopefully learned. When I left teaching and started selling land, it was as though I discovered a gold mine without having to do any of the backbreaking work. Yes, I worked, but I just did what felt right.

It took a brilliant psychologist, Dr. Robert Sternberg, to understand what that innate skill was, and to finally give it a name: *practical intelligence.* Dr. Sternberg noticed there are some people who have the ability to talk themselves into or out of any situation. They were natural problem-solvers. They would quickly learn from their environment, analyze what they needed to understand, and successfully apply their knowledge to any given task. This was their practical intelligence at work. And while it certainly provides a leg up for those who are born with it, the wonderful thing about practical intelligence is that it can be learned—that is, passed on to others. And while I call these skills street smarts, and have been teaching them for years, this practical intelligence can be the magic that changes your career as a salesperson.

At this point, hopefully you've read the book and understood the elements and tools that you will need to become a successful sales rep. However, knowing the various aspects of selling is not the same thing as putting them all together to be used successfully. Knowing and applying are two very different things.

Some of these skills may sound easy to you when first read. You may even have said to yourself after reading a chapter, "I knew that." But, for thirty-plus years, I have seen salespeople fail to reach their potential simply because they thought they knew it all. A few of these skills do look easy when first read. Believe me, they may look easy, but to use them in the real world of sales is not easy. It takes practice, it takes commitment, it takes street smart perseverance.

I know, too, that many of you will finish reading this page and close the book, saying it was a good book, but never implementing the tactics of the street smart sales pros. Others will say that they have seen the light and proceed to carry out many of my ideas for a week or two, and then fall back into their old patterns and habits of becoming a faker, taker, or maker. Don't let this happen to you. You read the book—now give yourself a chance to reach greatness. Don't put it on your bookshelf to gather dust.

Because each of us is unique, with different strengths and weaknesses, you must sit down and identify just what your weaknesses are, and then use the street smart sales pro's tools to correct the area in which you feel deficient. After working on your weaknesses, sit down and identify your strengths, and again use the street smart sales pro's tactics to make your strengths even more effective.

As I said at the end of Part One, the individual skills that you have learned are required if you are going to become a street smart sales pro; however, you can never get the results that you want until you put them together to run like a perfectly tuned motor.

Take this information and consider it for a while. Reread those sections that you have to work on, and then go for it!

Success can be yours if you simply do the right thing. The street smart sales pro knows this and now so do you. Gain the practical intelligence; and remember, the one who dies with the most toys wins. See you at your favorite toy store!

Resources

Books on Fear and Anxiety

Achor, Shawn. *The Happiness Advantage: The Seven Principles of Positive Psychology that Fuel Success and Performance at Work.* New York: Crown Business, 2010.

Bourne, Edmund J. *The Anxiety and Phobia Workbook.* Oakland, CA: New Harbinger Publications, 2011.

Desberg, Peter. *Speaking Scared, Sounding Good.* Garden City Park, NY: Square One Publishers, 2006.

Esposito, Janet E. *In The SpotLight, Overcome Your Fear of Public Speaking and Performing.* Bridgewater, CT: SpotLight LLC, 2005.

Jeffers, Susan. *Feel the Fear . . . and Do It Anyway.* New York: Ballantine Books, 2006.

Nhat Hanh, Thich. *Fear: Essential Wisdom for Getting Through the Storm.* New York: HarperOne, 2012.

Orloff, Judith. *Emotional Freedom: Liberate Yourself from Negative Emotions and Transform Your Life.* New York: Three Rivers Press, 2010.

Schaubb, Friedemann. *The Fear and Anxiety Solution: A Breakthrough Process for Healing and Empowerment with Your Subconscious Mind.* Louisville, CO: 2012.

Books on Selling

Carew, Jack. *You'll Never Get No for an Answer.* New York: Simon and Schuster, 1987.

Cialdini, Robert B. *Influence: The Psychology of Persuasion.* New York: William Morrow & Company, 1993.

Gayle, William. *Seven Seconds to Success in Selling.* Upper Saddle River, NJ: Prentice Hall, 1963.

Girard, Joe, and Stanley H. Brown. *How to Sell Anything to Anybody.* New York: Fireside, 2005.

Gitomer, Jeffrey. *The Sales Bible: The Ukltimate Sales Resource.* Hoboken, NJ: John Wiley & Sons, 2003.

Hopkins, Tom. *How to Master the Art of Selling.* New York: Business Plus, 2005.

Johnson, Spencer. *The One Minute Sales Person.* New York: HarperCollins, 2002.

Kaplan, Mike. *Secrets of a Master Closer: A Simpler, Easter, and Faster Way to Sell Anything.* Clearwater, FL: Oculus Publishers, 2012.

Tracy, Brian. *The Psychology of Selling: Increase Your Sales Faster and Easier than You Ever Thought Possible.* Nashville, TN: Thomas Nelson, 2006.

Ziglar, Zig. *Secrets of Closing the Sale.* Grand Rapids, MI: Fleming H. Revell, 2003.

Books on Success

Allen, David. *Getting Things Done: The Art of Stress-Free Productivity.* New York: Penguin Books, 2002.

Barber, Anne, and Lynne Waymon. *Make Your Contacts Count: Networkign Know-how for Business and Career Success.* New York: American Management Association, 2007.

Britt, Jim. *Do This, Get Rich! 12 Things You can Do Now to Gain Financial Freedom.* Garden City Park, NY: Square One Publishers.

Cabane, Olivia Fox. *The Charisma Myth: How Anyone Can Master the Art and Science of Personal Magnetism.* New York: Portfolio Trade Books, 2013.

Carnegie, Dale. *How to Win Friends and Influence People.* New York: Simon & Schuster, 2009.

Covey, Stephen R. *The 7 Habits of Highly Effective People: Powerful Lessons in Personal Change.* New York: Free Press, 2004.

Gladwell, Malcolm. *Blink: The Power of Thinking Without Thinking.* New York: Back Bay Books, 2007.

Gladwell, Malcolm. *Outliers: The Story of Success.* New York: Back Bay Books, 2011.

Gladwell, Malcolm. *The Tipping Point: How Little Things Can Make A Big Difference.* New York: Back Bay Books, 2002.

Kerpen, Dave. *How to Delight Your Customers, Create an Irresistible Brand, and Be Generally Amazing on Facebook (And Other Social Networks).* New York: McGraw Hill, 2011.

Salpeter, Miriam. *Social Networking for Career Success: Using Online Tools to Create a Personal Brand.* New York: LearningExpress, 2011.

Schuller, Robert. *Move Ahead with Possibility Thinking.* New York: Jove Books, 1978.

Seligman, Martin E.P. *Authentic Happiness: Using the New Positive Psychology to Realize Your Potential for Lasting Fulfillment.* New York: Atria Books, 2003.

Sternberg, Robert J. *Successful Intelligence: How Practical and Creative Intelligence Determine Success in Life.* New York: Plume Books, 1997.

Tolle, Eckhart. *The Power of Now: A Guide to Spiritual Enlightenment.* Novato, CA: New World Library, 1999.

Audiobooks and Podcasts on Public Speaking

Carnegie, Dale. *The Art of Public Speaking.* Read by Jason McCoy. Beverly Hills, CA: Big Happy Family, LLC, 2010. Audiobook, 4 hours and 38 minutes.

Miller, Fred Elliott. "'No Sweat' Public Speaking!" Podcast audio program. St. Louis, MO: No Sweat Public Speaking, 2011. https://itunes.apple.com/us/pod cast/no-sweat-public-speaking!/id426048931 (accessed May 23, 2013).

QuickandDirtyTips.com, "The Public Speaker's Quick and Dirty Tips for Improving Your Communication Skills." Podcast audio program. New York: Macmillan Holdings, 2013. https://itunes.apple.com/us/podcast/public-speakers-quick-dirty/id288508989 (accessed May 23, 2013).

Swisher, Margaret, and Barbara Myslik. "Overcoming Public Speaking Anxiety." Podcast audio program. Davis, CA: The Regents of University of California, Davis, 2011 https://itunes.apple.com/us/itunes-u/overcoming-public-speaking/id414117823 (accessed May 23, 2013).

Zeoli, Richard. *The Seven Principles of Public Speaking.* Read by Peter Johnson. Newark, NJ: Audible, Inc., 2013. Audiobook, 5 hours.

Courses On Public Speaking

Dale Carnegie Training
780 Third Avenue C-1
New York, NY 10017
(800) 231–5800
www.dalecarnegie.com
Educational institute with many franchise locations worldwide; courses focus on self-improvement and effective communication.

Speaking Circles
223 San Anselmo Avenue, Suite 6
San Anselmo, CA 94960
(414) 524-8353
www.speakingcircles.com
Community-based organization with locations in North America, Europe, and Asia; offers both public and private courses on communication.

Toastmasters International
23182 Arroyo Vista
Rancho Santa Margarita, CA 92688
(949) 858-8255
www.toastmasters.org
*Nonprofit educational organization
with many club locations worldwide;
devoted to improving public speaking
and leadership abilities.*

Fraternal Orders and Service Organizations

**Benevolent and Protective Order
  of the Elks**
National Memorial and
  Headquarters
2750 North Lakeview Avenue
Chicago, IL 60614
(773) 755-4700
www.elks.org
*Fraternal order that supports veteran
services, youth programs, and American
patriotism.*

Kiwanis International
3636 Woodview Trace
Indianapolis, IN 46268
(800) 549-2647 (dial 411)
http://sites.kiwanis.org/Kiwanis/en
  /home/aspx
*Service organization that supports a
variety of charitable causes, particularly
the welfare of children and youth.*

Lions Clubs International
300 West 22nd Street
Oak Brook, IL 60523
(630) 571-5466
www.lionsclubs.org

*Service organization that supports
a variety of charitable causes, with
a focus on initiatives for the blind
and visually impaired.*

Rotary International
One Rotary Center
1560 Sherman Avenue
Evanston, IL 60201
www.rotary.org
*Service organization that supports
a variety of charitable causes,
particularly health, literacy, youth,
and peace initiatives.*

Consumer-Based Guides to Businesses

Angie's List
1030 East Washington Street
Indianapolis, IN 46202
1-888-944-5478
www.angieslist.com
*Website with verified customer reviews
of service companies. Membership
required.*

Better Business Bureau
3033 Wilson Blvd, Suite 600
Arlington, VA 22201
(703) 276-0100
www.bbb.org
*Nonprofit consumer organization
featuring online evaluations of
local businesses and services.*

Yelp
www.yelp.com
*Website devoted to crowd-sourcing
reviews of local businesses and services.*

About the Author

Arthur Rogen has been involved with sales for over forty years. He began as a sales representative for United States Properties, earning the industry's highest sales performance award. He progressed to Divisional Sales Manager of the company's Eastern Marine Penn Properties division.

After leaving United States Properties, he successfully ran his own real estate development company. Seven years later, Arthur decided to sell off his interests to concentrate on his true love, teaching. For the next twelve years, he traveled throughout the country as a sales and marketing consultant for numerous companies. Having trained thousands of salespeople throughout the United States, Mr. Rogen took his formidable sales and marketing skills and, along with his wife, established a highly successful third-party medical examination company.

Mr. Rogen received his undergraduate degree from Rider College. His graduate work was completed at City College of New York.

Index

HOW TO READ A PERSON LIKE A BOOK

Observing Body Language to Know What People Are Thinking

Gerard I. Nierenberg, Henry H. Calero, and Gabriel Grayson

Imagine meeting someone for the first time and within minutes— without a word being said—having the ability to tell what that person is thinking. Magic? Not quite. Whether people are aware of it or not, their body movements clearly express their attitudes and motives, communicating key information that is invaluable in a range of situations.

How to Read a Person Like a Book will teach you how to interpret the nonverbal signals of business associates, friends, loved ones, and even strangers. Best-selling authors Nierenberg, Calero, and Grayson have put their working knowledge of body language into this practical guide to recognizing and understanding body movements. They share their proven techniques for gaining control of negotiations, detecting lies, and even recognizing signs of sexual attraction. You will discover how reading body language is a unique skill that offers real and important benefits.

$13.95 • 128 pages • 6 x 9-inch quality paperback • ISBN 978-0-7570-0314-1

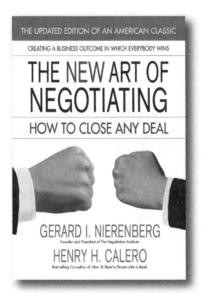

THE NEW ART OF NEGOTIATING

How to Close Any Deal

Gerard I. Nierenberg and Henry H. Calero

You negotiate every day of your life. Whether you are asking your employer for a raise or persuading your child to do his homework, everything is a negotiation. Written by Gerard Nierenberg, the world's foremost authority on the subject, *The New Art of Negotiating* is an updated, expanded version of the million-copy bestseller that introduced us all to the art of effective negotiation.

When *The Art of Negotiating* first appeared, it taught us that negotiation doesn't have to be an adversarial process that ends in victory for one party and defeat for his hapless rival. Since then, the landscape of business has changed greatly. *The New Art of Negotiating* provides Nierenberg's effective strategies redesigned for today's world. You will learn how to analyze your opponent's motivation, negotiate toward mutually satisfying terms, learn from your opponent's body language, and much more. Throughout, the author will guide you in successfully applying his famous "everybody wins" tactics to the bargaining process.

Once, Gerard Nierenberg changed the way we think about negotiating. Now, *The New Art of Negotiating* allows us to experience win-win success in today's business climate.

$15.95 • 256 pages • 6 x 9-inch quality paperback • ISBN 978-0-7570-0305-9

DO THIS, GET RICH!

12 Things You Can Do Now to Gain Financial Freedom

Jim Britt

Too many of us think that hard work and long hours are the keys to getting ahead. But Jim Britt knows that success is all about waking up the aspiring entrepreneur within you—about taking control. And it's about knowing what steps to take to achieve true financial freedom.

Do This. Get Rich! is a straightforward guide that offers twelve simple yet powerful tools for achieving financial success. You will not only gain the skills needed to build and succeed in your own business, but you will win a new sense of direction and confidence that will guide you in reaching your most ambitious goals. You will also have a practical framework from which to handle everyday personal and business challenges, as well as strategies needed in today's business world.

An American success story, Jim Britt pulled himself out of poverty and went on to make his fortune in the world of business. Wishing to share his secrets of success with others, he then began to lecture. To date, his seminars have attracted over one million attendees. Jim Britt is also the man who gave Tony Robbins his first real job--a job that would inspire Tony to gain his own financial freedom. *Do This. Get Rich!* is not just a title, but a pledge that the author has made to you, and that you can make to yourself.

$25.95 • 216 pages • 6 x 9-inch hardback • ISBN 978-0-7570-0241-0

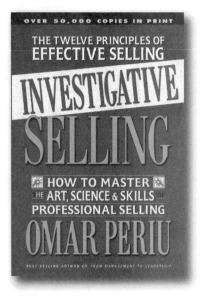

INVESTIGATIVE SELLING

How to Master the Art, Science & Skills of Professional Selling

Omar Periu

Within each super salesperson is an expert detective as skilled as Sherlock Holmes. For a lucky few, these sleuthing talents come naturally, but for most, these skills must be learned—and it is these skills that turn the average salesperson into the master seller. Now, Omar Periu, nationally renowned "high energy" sales trainer, provides readers with the secrets of becoming a top sales professional in *Investigative Selling*.

Like any good investigation, selling begins with observation, questioning, and listening. *Investigative Selling* not only details these skills, but also explains the most effective way to use the information you gather. And it applies investigative selling techniques to a range of sales activities, from prospecting to presenting to closing.

Could your sales skills be improved? If the answer is yes, this is the "how to" book you need to read now.

$15.95 • 240 pages • 6 x 9-inch quality paperback • ISBN 978-0-7570-0285-4